Praise for *uncovered editions*

"The repackaging o̶ ... ...̶im Coates has come up ... ...ng of history. His uncov... ...of The Stationery Offi... ...n UFOs in the House ... ...ation, directly from Hansard, of a nu... ...took place in 1979 ... This is inspired publishing, not only archivally valuable but capable of bringing the past back to life without the usual filter of academic or biographer." **Guardian**

"The Irish Uprising is a little treasure of a book and anyone with an interest in Irish history will really enjoy it. Its structure is extremely unusual as it is compiled from historic official reports published by the British government from 1914 to 1920 ... For anyone studying this period of history The Irish Uprising is a must as the correspondence and accounts within it are extremely illuminating and the subtle nuances of meaning can be teased out of the terms and phrasing to be more revelatory than the actual words themselves." **Irish Press, Belfast**

"Voyeurs of all ages will enjoy the original text of the Denning report on Profumo. It is infinitely superior to the film version of the scandal, containing such gems as: 'One night I was invited to a dinner party at the home of a very, very rich man. After I arrived, I discovered it was rather an unusual dinner party. All the guests had taken off their clothes ... The most intriguing person was a man with a black mask over his face. At first I thought this was a party gimmick. But the truth was that this man is so well known and holds such a responsible position that he did not want to be associated with anything improper.'" **Times Higher Education Supplement**

"Very good to read ... insight into important things ... inexorably moving ... If you want to read about the Titanic, you won't read a better thing ... a revelation." **Open Book, BBC Radio 4**

"Congratulations to The Stationery Office for unearthing and reissuing such an enjoyable vignette" [on Wilfrid Blunt's Egyptian Garden] **The Spectator**

uncovered editions
www.uncovered-editions.co.uk

Series editor: Tim Coates
Managing editor: Michele Staple

New titles in the series

Already published

uncovered editions

THE ST VALENTINE'S DAY MASSACRE, 1929

FBI FILES RELATING TO THE MURDER OF SEVEN MEMBERS OF THE BUGS MORAN GANG ON 14 FEBRUARY 1929

∘◦◦⬥◦◦∘

London: The Stationery Office

© The Stationery Office 2001

Applications for reproduction should be made in writing to The Stationery Office Limited, St Crispins, Duke Street, Norwich NR3 1PD.

ISBN 0 11 702749 9
Extracts taken from the files of the Federal Bureau of Investigation, available under the Freedom of Information Act.

A CIP catalogue record for this book is available from the British Library.

Cover photograph of Italian-American gangster Al Capone with US Marshal Laubenheimer © Hulton Archive.

Typeset by J&L Composition Ltd, Filey, North Yorkshire.
Printed in the United Kingdom by The Stationery Office, London.
TJ4553 C30 9/01

CONTENTS

About the series

Uncovered editions are historic official papers which have not previously been available in a popular form, and have been chosen for the quality of their story-telling. Some subjects are familiar, but others are less well known. Each is a moment in history.

About the series editor, Tim Coates

Tim Coates studied at University College, Oxford and at the University of Stirling. After working in the theatre for a number of years, he took up bookselling and became managing director, firstly of Sherratt and Hughes bookshops, and then of Waterstone's. He is known for his support for foreign literature, particularly from the Czech Republic. The idea for *uncovered editions* came while searching through the bookshelves of his late father-in-law, Air Commodore Patrick Cave, OBE. He is married to Bridget Cave, has two sons, and lives in London.

Tim Coates welcomes views and ideas on the *uncovered editions* series. He can be e-mailed at tim.coates@theso.co.uk

The cold-blooded murder of seven members of the Bugs Moran gang on 14 February 1929 was the high-water mark in organised crime during the Prohibition era (1919–33) in the USA. There was intense rivalry for control of the illegal traffic in alcohol, with gangsters engaged in large-scale smuggling, manufacture and sale. When "business" takeovers and mergers failed, the gangsters would wipe out the competition with guns.

Selected files on the St Valentine's Day massacre from the Federal Bureau of Investigation (FBI) are reproduced here. No prosecution was brought at the time of the murders by the Chicago Police Department, and, in 1929, there was no violation of federal law that would allow the FBI to investigate. So the file begins in 1935.

Law enforcement in the US has traditionally been the responsibility of state and local governments. However, crimes that come under federal jurisdiction (such as those committed in more than one state) are the responsibility of the FBI. The bureau also provides help in the form of fingerprint identification and other technical laboratory services.

Please note that spellings of some names are inconsistent in the original documents. Also, some of the original documents were not dated, and therefore the contents may occasionally be out of chronological sequence.

BREAKING NEWS, JANUARY 1935

[*Chicago American*, January 23, 1935]

BOLTON NAMES SELF AND FIVE OTHERS AS ST VALENTINE KILLERS

1, Humphreys; 2, Burke; 3, Maddox; 4, Bolton; 5, Winkler; 6, Goetz

The seven men killed in the infamous St Valentine's Day massacre—the greatest crime in Chicago gang annals—were massacred by Fred ("Killer") Burke, Claude Maddox, Byron Bolton,

Gus Winkler, Fred Goetz and Murray Humphreys.

That is the story of Byron Bolton. He states that the actual machine gunners were himself, Maddox, Humphreys and Winkler. He named Burke and Goetz as the two "policemen", armed with sawn-off shotguns, whom witnesses reported seeing at the North Clark Street garage after the mass murders.

Bolton has given his story in a detailed formal statement to the United States government. It is now being studied by high officials. Meanwhile, however, he also had told it to Chicago friends. And it is from them that the *Chicago American* obtained the story.

Bolton was captured January 8 in a spectacular raid on his apartment hideout at 3820 Pine Grove Avenue in which Russell Gibson was killed by federal agents. He now is in St Paul in connection with the Bremer $200,000 ransom kidnapping in which he is alleged to have participated.

Bolton, before he entered crime to share in the profits of bootlegging, was an expert machine gunner in the US Navy. It was there, according to his story, that he gained the knowledge which enabled him to handle so deftly one of the four roaring weapons which spat wholesale death on February 14, 1929.

The seven who were killed on that day were Peter Gusenberg, ex-convict; Frank Gusenberg, his brother; Adam Heyer alias Arthur Hayes, ex-convict; James Clark, brother of George ("Bugs") Moran, North Side gang leader at the time; John May, garage mechanic; Albert Weinshank and Reinhardt H. Schwimmer.

May was a youth who was a victim of circumstances who was working in the garage at the time the murderers entered. Schwimmer associated with gangsters for the "kick" he got out of it. The others were all members of Moran's gang, which then was fighting Al Capone's mobsters.

Bolton's story traced the massacre to New York and the avarice of Frank Uale, notorious eastern gangster. Uale, he said, coveted a "piece" of a dog track operating with Capone's backing in Lyons, Illinois.

[*Washington Post*, January 24, 1935]

GANG MASSACRE VALENTINE DAY IS HELD SOLVED

Chicago reports suspect confessed, implicating five others in crime

Chicago, Jan. 23 (Associated Press). Reports were published here today that the underworld's most gory crime—the 1929 Valentine Day massacre of seven gangsters—had been solved by the statement of Byron Bolton, held as a member of the notorious Karpis–Barker mob.★

The *Chicago American*, in a copyrighted story, said Bolton had named all participants in the crime and that his written statement was now in the hands of J. Edgar Hoover, head of the Division of Investigation of the Department of Justice at Washington.

Dissemination of the story brought immediate and conflicting statements. Said Hoover: "There's not a word of truth in it." Said Police Capt. John Stege, underworld authority of the Chicago force: "It sounds probable." Said D. M. Ladd, agent in charge at the Chicago Division of Investigation: "Federal agents have not questioned Bolton about the massacre."

Named as "trigger men" and plotters in the massacre by Bolton, the *American* said, were: Murray Humphreys, one time No. 1 man of the Capone mob, now serving a term in Leavenworth for income tax evasion; Claude Maddox, hoodlum still at large; Fred ("Killer") Burke, serving time in Michigan for murder; Gus Winkler, slain underworld go-between; Fred ("The Brains") Goetz, university man turned gangster, and Bolton.

Slain in efforts to exterminate the George ("Bugs") Moran gang on Valentine Day were Peter

---

★ The Karpis–Barker gang comprised Kate "Ma" Barker, her sons (Herman, Lloyd, Arthur and Fred), Alvin Karpis and other criminals.

Gusenberg, former convict; Frank, his brother; Adam Heyer, alias Arthur Hayes, former convict; James Clark, brother-in-law of Moran; John May, garage mechanic; Albert Weinshank, and Dr Reinhardt H. Schwimmer.

The whole plot was a story of the familiar "double-cross", the effort of Al Capone to maintain control of a dog track at Lyons, Illinois, which one of his affiliates, Frank Uale, Chicago and New York gangster, coveted. Uale was reported to have thrown his allegiance to Moran, North Side leader, in attempts to "cut in" on the dog track and Capone hired "Killer" Burke and others to protect his interest.

Moran's headquarters were in a North Clark Street garage. For days Bolton was reported to have watched the place and then given the alarm when he saw Moran's cohorts enter, Moran with them. The killers entered, two dressed in police uniforms, unlimbered machine guns, lined up their victims, and blazed away. Moran disappeared and has since "retired."

Arrests and alibis followed and no solution was forthcoming, although at that time Police Lieut. Frank Cusack said ballistics tests pointed to Bolton, former Navy machine gunner.

Meanwhile, the hunt for Alvin Karpis, desperate co-leader of the Karpis-Barker gang wanted for the $200,000 kidnapping of Edward G. Bremer, St Paul banker, centered in the Midwest as federal agents, police and sheriffs' officers by the hundred followed every slim clue and report.

Sunday, Karpis and his trigger-crazed pal, Harry Campbell, shot their way through a police trap in Atlantic City, stole an automobile and escaped. Since then they zoomed their way toward the Midwest, stealing cars and kidnapping the owners temporarily.

Today two roughly dressed men in an automobile bearing Ohio license plates overpowered two bank officials and two customers at the Trivoli (Illinois) state bank near Peoria and escaped with nearly $3,000. Authorities saw the possibility of the desperate hand of Karpis and Campbell in that crime.

Yesterday Karpis and Campbell abandoned a Pennsylvania doctor's car near Monroe, Michigan, after releasing the doctor in Ohio on their flight. They were next reported seen near Pontiac, Michigan, and state police combed that area.

Chicago police, with "shoot to kill" orders from Detective Chief John L. Sullivan, expected the pair to head for Chicago for one of their numerous hideouts. All entrances to the metropolis were scanned minutely.

Karpis and Campbell are the only two of the important members of the gang sought for the Bremer kidnapping still at large. Fred Barker and his mother, Kate (Ma) Barker, were slain by federal agents in a protracted gun battle in Florida;

Fred's brother, Arthur, is in custody at St Paul; Bolton also has been taken there, and Gibson went to the end of the criminal one-way street— death.

[*Washington Herald*, January 24, 1935]

PRISONER CLAIMS HE SLEW SEVEN IN VALENTINE MASSACRE

Chicago, Jan. 23 (Universal Service). Authorities investigating the story circulated here today that Byron Bolton had named himself and five others as the killers in the famous St Valentine Day massacre in 1929, tonight expressed doubt it was true, almost at the same time that J. Edgar Hoover of the Department of Justice labeled the tale as "bunk".

Bert M. Massee, foreman of the coroner's jury that remained intact two years investigating the crime that cost the lives of seven "Bugs" Moran gangsters, said:

> I do not recall the name of Bolton ever being
> mentioned, but other names attributed to Bolton
> have been published frequently in connection with
> the slaying.

Bolton, at St Paul, where he is held as a money passer in connection with the kidnapping of Edward G. Bremer, was arrested here two weeks ago when federal agents killed his partner, Russell Gibson, in a raid on their apartment.

Authorities pointed out that Bolton may be attempting to have himself returned to this state for trial in connection with the slayings, hoping in the meantime for some avenue of escape, in order to defeat the federal kidnapping prosecution which is almost certain to send him to prison.

The Valentine Day massacre occurred before the noon hour. Two men disguised as policemen drove up to the North Clark Street garage and entered, holding the seven men in custody and making them line up, facing the wall. Four other men entered bearing machine guns and mowed them down.

Only a pet dog survived. Bolton in his tale, claimed he was one of the machine-gunners.

[*Washington Star*]

REPORT OF BOLTON BREAK IS DENIED

US officials deny confession of St Valentine's Day massacre

Chicago, Jan. 23. D. M. Ladd, agent in charge of the Division of Investigation, Department of Justice, denied a published story today that Byron Bolton, Karpis-Barker gangster, had made any statement admitting participation in the 1929 St Valentine's Day massacre, in which seven were slain.

Ladd issued a formal statement in which he denied that Bolton had made any such admission, written or oral. He said further that federal agents had not questioned Bolton about the massacre because it was not in their jurisdiction, and that Chicago police authorities had not questioned Bolton after his arrest. He said that since Bolton was taken to St Paul, he has remained in federal custody, intimating that local authorities there could not have questioned him.

FBI Correspondence, January 23, 1935

Memorandum for the Director

Time 2.15 pm

Kindly be informed that Mr Carusi telephoned and stated that information had been received indicating the *Chicago American* was about to publish a story that Byron Bolton, a member of the Karpis-Barker gang, has allegedly made a confession to the St Valentine's Day massacre and has implicated a Fred Burke, Gus Winkler, Humphreys, and several others and that the confession of Bolton was in the Department being carefully studied; that the other newspaper reporters are frantic and Mr Carusi states that he would like to have some word on this matter either confirming or denying, stating that the other reporters have intimated that it seems very strange the *Chicago American* is able to get information in advance.

I informed him that I had no knowledge of the matter mentioned above, but would gladly call it to your attention.

T.D. QUINN
Division of Investigation
US Department of Justice
Washington DC

Memorandum for the Director

Time 2.45 pm
Mr Ladd telephoned and advised that the *Chicago American* was carrying a story to the effect that Byron Bolton had given out information which cleared up the St Valentine Day massacre in Chicago. Mr Ladd advised that Bolton had not given out any information concerning this while he was being questioned in Chicago and that as far as he, Mr Ladd, knew, the story was false; further that he had refused to make any comment to other newspapers concerning this story.

I advised Mr Ladd that I would submit this information to you.

Time 2.50 pm

I telephoned Mr Ladd and advised him that upon receiving the above information, you desired to have Mr Ladd first ascertain from Mr Nathan at St Paul that Bolton did not make such a statement there and then he, Mr Ladd, should issue a statement at Chicago denying the information published in the *Chicago American*, stating that no such statement had been secured from Bolton.

Time 4.15 pm

Mr Ladd telephoned from Chicago and advised that he had issued the statement to the newspapers denying that Bolton had given any information to the Division regarding the St Valentine's Day massacre. Mr Ladd advised that he had first ascertained definitely from Mr Nathan at St Paul that Bolton had made no such statement there.

Time 4.20 pm

I telephoned Mr Nathan at St Paul and stated it was your wish that no one, other than Bolton's attorney, should be permitted to see Bolton; that it was probable that the various newspapers would be wanting to interview him as a result of the story appearing in the *Chicago American*, but that this should not be permitted. Mr Nathan stated that instructions had already been issued to the effect that no one should be permitted to see Bolton without prior authority from the St Paul Division office.

E.A. Tamm
Division of Investigation
US Department of Justice
Washington DC

Memorandum for Mr Tamm

Time 6.26 pm
Mr Carusi telephoned and stated that the press, in quoting any denial of Byron Bolton's connection with the above matter, seems to differ somewhat as to my conception of the same.

I told him that while none of the press representatives had talked to me about it, Col. Gates had telephoned and I absolutely denied that Byron Bolton made any statements or confessions relative to the above matter.

John Edgar Hoover
Director
Division of Investigation
US Department of Justice
Washington DC

[*Miami Daily News* and *New York Post*, January 24, 1935]

GANG MASSACRE—FINGER POINTS TOWARD CAPONE

Murder charge against former crime overlord is thought possible

Chicago, Jan. 24 (AP). Seven dead men, victims of the St Valentine's Day massacre, cast a shadow today over the possible fate of Al Capone. From graves where they have lain since 1929, the victims of Chicago's bloodiest crime were said in reports published here to be the most serious threat to the former gang lord's safety since his conviction on a federal income tax evasion charge.

The *Herald and Examiner* stated that Byron Bolton, held in St Paul charged with a part in the Bremer kidnapping, had confessed as "finger man"* for the mass slaying and had named the actual slayers, listing five names familiar in underworld haunts. Though US government officials were quick to deny they had a confession, the newspaper said federal officers were hopeful of tracing those seven murders down to the original public enemy No. 1, Al Capone, now in Alcatraz prison.

---

* Police informer, grass.

The report quoted Bolton as attributing the massacre to henchmen hired by Capone to protect his interests in a Lyons, Illinois, dog race track after the George (Bugs) Moran gang and Frank Uale, New York and Chicago gangster, attempted to "muscle in" on the profits.

Those named as killers, who left their quarry in a blood-spattered garage in February, 1929, were: Murray Humphreys, once No. 1 Capone man, now in Leavenworth on an income tax evasion conviction; Fred (Killer) Burke, serving a term in a Michigan prison for slaying a St Joseph policeman; Gus Winkler, North Side gambler killed a year ago; Claude Maddox, leader of the extinct Circus gang, the only one now at large, and Fred (The Brains) Goetz, University of Illinois graduate, who turned gangster. Goetz was slain last year.

Reports said that Bolton, taken in a raid here on January 10, the night federal bullets slew Russell Gibson, Karpis–Barker gangster, confessed he was the man who rented a room opposite the Clark Street garage and gave the signal when the Moran mobsters arrived at their headquarters.

The *Herald and Examiner* pointed out that, should a case be developed against Capone, the federal government might turn the former bootleg king over to the state for prosecution on a murder charge when his 10-year term for tax evasion and one year for contempt are completed. And others implicated might be brought from their prison cells to face prosecution for the gory murders that were credited with focusing attention of the federal government on the menace of Chicago's war lords.

Following the murders, police sought the slayers. Arrests were made, but the alibis brought freedom though ballistics experts said evidence pointed to Bolton, a former Navy machine-gunner. Burke and Maddox were also listed by police at the time as suspects.

The crime has been listed five years as an unsolved mystery.

[*Chicago Herald and Examiner*, January 24, 1935]

TALE MAY SEND CAPONE TO CHAIR

St Valentine confession accuses first "Public Enemy No. 1"

Al Capone, former Chicago gang lord, now in prison, ordered the Moran mob "wiped out", according to the confession of Byron Bolton yesterday.

Through the purported confession of Byron Bolton that he and five others perpetrated Chicago's ghastliest crime—the St Valentine's Day massacre of 1929—federal officials yesterday were said to be hopeful of pinning those seven murders on Al Capone, America's original Public Enemy No. 1.

This, if successful, would take Capone from Alcatraz, where he is serving eleven years for income tax evasion, and head him toward the electric chair.

Bolton revealed for the first time that Terry Druggan, the famous fashion-plate* beer peddler, came within seconds of dying in the massacre.

Although Department of Justice officials emphatically denied that Bolton had made such a confession, it was recalled that the department's policy has been to refuse to admit possession of evidence.

[*St Paul Daily Times*, January 24, 1935]

CAPONE MAY BE TRIED FOR "MASSACRE" AS HENCHMAN CONFESSES

Chicago, Jan. 24. Alphonse Capone, imprisoned gang overlord, may be brought from Alcatraz island penitentiary to answer for the ghastly St Valentine's Day massacre of seven Moran gangsters here in 1929.

This possibility loomed today following the disclosure by International News Service that Byron Bolton, now a federal prisoner, had made a detailed statement of the massacre to Department

---

* Fashion-plate: someone who always wears the latest fashions.

of Justice agents. Bolton and five others were named as the killers.

While police officials began to reshuffle their scanty evidence in the gruesome mass murder, federal officials were said to be hopeful of linking Capone to the crime with the object of sending him to the electric chair, if possible.

Those named as the actual murderers who lined up seven of George (Bugs) Moran's gang against a North Clark Street garage wall and mowed them down with machine gun fire were known to be affiliates of the Capone mob, then engaged in a war for supremacy against Moran's men.

They were Murray Humphreys, Gus Winkler, Fred (Killer) Burke, Claude Maddox and Fred Goetz. Humphreys, who succeeded Capone to the gangland throne, is now in prison at Leavenworth, Kansas. Burke is serving a life term at Marquette (Michigan) penitentiary. Winkler and Goetz were murdered and only Maddox, leader of the "Circus" gang, Capone affiliate, is at large.

As police authorities dug back into their investigation new evidence was brought to light. Bolton's brother, John, had been sought as a participant in the massacre, police announced. So had John Conroy, found slain in New York in 1932.

Bolton, in his confession, said he was one of the killers. Police had been trailing the former Egan's Rats gangster as the man who conducted the death watch in a rented room across the street from the massacre garage. He was first connected with the crime when a letter addressed to him and postmarked from Thayer, Illinois, was found in the abandoned room.

Conroy, it was disclosed by Detective Frank Morell, was also known as Robert Newberry. When Burke was first linked to the St Valentine Day murders, a search for Conroy, one of Burke's henchmen, was begun. The hunt ended when Conroy was found dead in a New York flat, Morrell said.

Bolton is now in federal custody at St Paul, as a suspect in the £200,000 kidnapping of Edward G. Bremer, a wealthy banker.

[*Chicago Tribune*, January 24, 1935]

POLICE TELL NEW SECRETS OF 1929 GANG MASSACRE

Pick flaws in reported Bolton confession

New evidence uncovered in the investigation of the St Valentine's Day massacre of seven north side gangsters came to light last night on the heels of published reports that Byron Bolton, now a federal prisoner, has made a full confession naming himself as one of the killers.

Despite the fact of emphatic denials from Department of Justice agents that Bolton made a confession, either written or oral, and despite the fact that the new evidence tended to disprove many details of the purported confession, the reports persisted that it had been made.

The new stories of the investigation of the massacre of the George (Bugs) Moran gangsters brought to light the fact that Bolton's brother, John, also had been sought for participation in the crime, as had John Conroy, who was found dead in a New York flat two years ago.

Since shortly after February 14, 1929, Byron Bolton had been sought as one of two men who rented a room across the street from the garage headquarters of the Moran gang at 2122 North Clark Street.

There he is supposed to have watched for an opportunity to catch Moran and his entire gang in the garage at one time, then call for the gangland executioners.

Bolton was linked with this role when a letter addressed to him and postmarked from Thayer, Illinois, was found in the room. At that time policeman Frank Morrell, assigned to the investigation, made a trip to Thayer. He found Bolton's parents, obtained a picture, and discovered that Bolton had been in the Navy during the war. The picture later was identified as that of the man who rented the room where the death watch was kept.

Bolton's trail led next to St Louis, the town where both he and Burke got their starts with the Egan's Rats gang. It was in St Louis, apparently, that

Bolton became associated with the Arthur Barker-Alvin Karpis gang, now blamed for the $200,000 kidnapping of Edward G. Bremer.

Bolton was finally captured in an apartment at 3820 Pine Grove Avenue, where a companion, Russell Gibson, wanted in the Bremer kidnapping, was killed attempting to shoot his way out of the government trap.

According to the purported confession, Bolton admitted renting the "death watch" room and occupying it as police had suspected, but he did not mention his brother. In addition, the report had it, Bolton joined the actual slayers when they entered the garage, and fired one of the machine guns.

Burke and Goetz, according to the reputed confession, were the two men dressed as police-men. They were chosen, Bolton is reported to have said, because they were not known to the Moran gang. Believing them real officers on a routine raid, the Moran men calmly allowed themselves to be disarmed and lined up against the wall.

Then came the blast from machine guns and shotguns that left dead on the floor Pete Gusenberg, Adam Heyer, James Clark, John May, Albert Weinshank and Dr Reinhardt H. Schwimmer. Frank Gusenberg was alive when police came, but died within a few hours.

The motive for the slaying, as Bolton is reported to have told it, involved the hiring of Frankie Uale, New York gang leader, by the North

Siders to aid in the war against Al Capone over operations of a dog track in Lyons, Illinois.

There, police found the first main flaw in the reputed Bolton confession. It was pointed out that Uale was slain in New York on July 1, 1928, nearly eight months before the massacre took place.

In addition, policeman Morrell, who spent many months in his investigation, declared that he never had heard the names of Humphreys or Maddox connected with the actual massacre.

Burke, Goetz and Winkler had been regarded as likely suspects, he said, and in addition, two other men were mentioned. They are John, the brother of Byron Bolton, and Robert Conroy, who was found dead in a New York flat in 1932.

Conroy, whose real name was Robert Newberry, was sought in 1929 as a member of Burke's gang, and one of the participants in the massacre itself. Policeman Morrell pointed out that if Byron Bolton made a confession, it was extremely likely that Conroy's name would have been mentioned.

As to whether Bolton could be expected to name his own brother, policeman Morrell would not say, but declared that all the evidence pointed to the fact that John Bolton was the second man in the room across from the garage.

Byron Bolton now is in St Paul, in federal custody, and was called as a witness before the federal Grand Jury reported to have voted indictments against three members of the Barker-Karpis gang, charging them with the Bremer abduction.

Harold Nathan, assistant to J. Edgar Hoover, chief of the Division of Investigation of the Department of Justice, sent vigorous denials from St Paul that Bolton had made a confession of the massacre. Mr Hoover sent a similar denial from Washington. In Chicago police officials said that they had not been informed of such a confession.

[*Chicago American*]

KILLER SAVED FROM GUNS OF FOES

Lieut. Otto Erlanson, veteran head of the police homicide squad, declared today he believes Byron Bolton's sensational story of the 1929 St Valentine's Day septuple gang massacre "is true in every line" as printed exclusively in the *Chicago American*.

Lieut. Erlanson went to work on the amazing case within a matter of minutes after the seven adherents of George ("Bugs") Moran were found slaughtered by machine gun fire in the gang garage headquarters at 2122 North Clark Street.

Today he had finished examining a huge box of massacre records and declared:

> I believe the *Chicago American*'s story is correct in every line from my investigation, which started right after the murders. When Bolton was arrested January

8 in the raid when Russell Gibson was killed by
federal men, I recalled at once that he was constantly
mentioned in our investigation.

It was while in federal custody after the January 8
raid on an apartment hideout at 3820 Pine Grove
Avenue, that Bolton told to government agents the
full story of the massacre, admitting that he was one
of the four machine gun killers.

The government is carefully guarding Bolton's
formal statement but friends of the gangster, to
whom he previously had told the story, revealed it
exclusively to the *Chicago American*.

In that story, Bolton described the four
machine gunners as having been himself, Claude
Maddox, Gus Winkler and Murray Humphreys.
Fred ("Killer") Burke and Fred Goetz, he added,
posed as policemen in full uniform to set the stage
for the carnage.

Chief of Detectives Sullivan displayed intense
interest in Bolton's story and said: "It sounds
plausible and has all the earmarks of being true."
He planned to confer today with Commissioner
of Police Allman to make plans for bringing
Bolton back to Chicago should he escape conviction in the $200,000 Edward G. Bremer
kidnapping in St Paul, for which he faces almost
certain indictment.

Chief Sullivan said the government refused
police permission to take Bolton to the detective

bureau for questioning before he was taken to St Paul, although an offer was made from police to quiz him in the Bankers' Building offices of the Division of Investigation, Department of Justice.

Lieut. Erlanson recalled that a woman living across the street from the Moran garage rented to a mysterious stranger a room fronting on Clark Street, with an unobstructed view of the garage front. That room, it was established soon after the massacre, was used as a watching post. Bolton, in his story, described himself as its tenant.

Lieut. Erlanson declared today the landlady at the time described her roomer in a manner that tallied with Bolton's description. Also, a letter addressed to Bolton from his old hometown of Thayer, Illinois, was found in the room, definitely linking him with the case.

Bolton's explanation of the "policemen" roles played by Burke and Goetz, who were unknown to the Moran gang, to gain entry without suspicion to the garage, also is borne out by his information, the police officer said.

Lieut. Erlanson recalled that the night after the massacre a large Cadillac touring car, identical with those used by detective bureau squads at that time, was found practically destroyed in a Cicero prairie. The automobile had been drenched with gasoline, set afire and bombed. Only the chassis remained. Serial numbers had been filed away, Lieut. Erlanson said, but science managed to reproduce them so that the car was traced through the hands of several dealers and owners—including Maddox, who then headed the murderous "Circus Gang" of the Northwest Side.

Lieut. Erlanson said Maddox was questioned, having at once fallen under suspicion, but glibly explained away the automobile angle.

Burke has always intrigued his interest, the officer said, but he has never been able definitely to hook the notorious killer to the crime. He declared today: "If Burke would talk the whole case would be cleared up."

Burke is serving a sentence of hard labor in the Michigan prison at Marquette for murdering a St Joseph, Michigan, policeman.

When arrested at St Joseph for the policeman's murder some months later, Burke's young wife, the innocent daughter of a small farmer, declared Burke and Bolton were close friends and frequently took trips together to Great Falls, Minnesota, and elsewhere.

The *Chicago American* also learned that Bolton barely beat the guns of gangland when he revealed the details of Chicago's most spectacular crime. To seal his lips Bolton's erstwhile underworld confederates had been waiting with weapons primed and cocked until the time was ripe. Bolton, they argued, was a sick man, always loquacious, and a man who has wanted to talk for some time. Instead, they either dallied too long or were unable to locate their target and the record of that gory crime has been put down in black and white through the story spilled from Bolton's own lips.

[*Chicago American*, January 24, 1935]

MASSACRE'S CIVIC PROBERS HAIL BOLTON EXPOSÉ

Earlier facts check with confession

After the massacre of seven hoodlum members of the "Bugs" Moran gang on St Valentine's Day, seven years ago, a rise of civic indignation gave birth to a coroner's jury of prominent leading Chicago citizens.

And today the members of that jury, who spent thousands of dollars of their own money to wipe the stigma of gangdom from Chicago, were emphatic in their belief that Byron Bolton's story of the real slaying as said to have been told to Department of Justice agents, was the first real word picture of the massacre.

It was the massacre that led to the establishment of the North-western Crime Detection Laboratory.

It was the massacre that first brought to the Middle West the use of ballistics in the scientific detection of crime.

Bolton's story, as published exclusively yesterday in the *Chicago American*, was told, his friends say, only because he had "gone soft". But the members of the coroner's jury who spent months in questioning of witnesses, covering more than 5,000 closely typed pages of testimony, declare that his story rings true. Burt A. Massee, prominent Chicagoan and foreman of the jury said:

> He seems to have a pretty good knowledge of the whole affair doesn't he? I don't recall having run across the name of Bolton in the actual slaying, but I do know that Burke was definitely connected as a suspect. We proved that with Col. Calvin Goddard's ballistics test of the spent shells.

Praise for the first real story of the slaying was offered to the *Chicago American* today by Walter W. L. Meyer, assistant to the Probate Judge of Cook County and a noted teacher of criminal law. He said:

> This is a wonderful exposé after so many years. I'm inclined to believe that Burke was connected with the shooting and I think that Bolton might have had something to do with it. I know Burke was connected with the anti-Moran Gang but I don't know just where Capone comes in. Bolton tells a good, well-connected story.

Felix Streyckmans, former newspaperman and practicing Chicago attorney who was a member of the jury, said:

> There are some phases of the story that I don't think are quite accurate. We definitely established the fact that only two machine guns were used, although Bolton claims that four men carried them. However, it is possible that only two of the gun carriers were the actual murderers. We traced the shotgun shells to two guns and afterward located them in Burke's home.

Dr John V. McCormick, member of the jury and dean of the Loyola University law school, said:

> Bolton's hook-up with Burke is fairly certain. I first heard Bolton's name mentioned in the slaying about three months after the inquest, but I can't remember in what connection. If Bolton didn't take part in the shooting, I don't see why he has confessed that he did.

Col. Albert A. Sprague blamed Bolton's conscience for his confession to the federal men. He said:

> I can't imagine what would move a man like Bolton to make such a confession, unless his conscience was bothering him. His name never came into the

inquest, but that did not mean anything particularly, because we spent most of our time in endeavoring to trace the bullets found in the bodies.

[*Chicago Daily Times*]

"CONFESSION" IN MASSACRE STIRS US OFFICIALS

Bolton story receiving serious consideration by department

Washington DC, Jan. 24. Publication of "confessions", attributed to Department of Justice sources, was receiving the attention of high officials of the department here today.

Officials of the department, whose agents are noted for their refusal to talk for publication, were irritated at reports published in Chicago that Byron Bolton, Barker-Karpis gangsters indicted in the Bremer kidnapping at St Paul today, had "confessed" the St Valentine Day massacre, naming five other hoodlums as his aids in the mass murder of seven Moran gangsters.

Bolton's confession to agents on file in the Department of Justice quarters in Washington does not mention the St Valentine Day massacre, officials said flatly today.

In view of the fact that the department, according to officials, obtained no statement, oral or written, from Bolton in which the St Valentine Day massacre was so much mentioned, the officials were seeking to trace the origin of the story.

From time to time there have been slight "leaks" in the Department of Justice offices at Chicago, and while yesterday's report was simply an irritant, the other situation has aroused grave concern on the part of officials and a determined effort to halt such "leaks" is under way.

The secrecy with which the department conducts its work, while admirable in many respects, observers point out, together with their agents' policy of announcing "I have nothing to say," makes the department peculiarly vulnerable in the matter of denials when an unfounded article is published.

Attorney-General Homer S. Cummings, in discussing Bolton's indictment at St Paul today, branded as "completely erroneous" the published report of his "massacre confession."

FBI Correspondence, January 24, 1935

Memoranda for Mr Tamm

Time 10.42 am
Colonel Gates telephonically made inquiry concerning the truth of a statement carried by Universal Service to the effect that I said that I had not heard that Bolton confessed his part in the St Valentine's Day massacre. I stated that it was not

correct; that the only comment I had made was that Bolton said that he did not know anything about the St Valentine's Day massacre; and that the story appearing in the *Chicago American* concerning the matter was one hundred percent incorrect.

Time 10.44 am

I telephoned Mr Ladd at the Chicago office and told him that I was very much concerned over the complaints which had been coming in, even before yesterday, from the other Chicago newspapers relative to the *Chicago American* and the stories their reporters get the "scoops" on. I stated that the *Chicago American* had the wrong "scoop" yesterday; that the other Chicago papers quote me as saying that there wasn't any truth in the article in the *Chicago American*; and that these papers quote him, Mr Ladd, as saying he had never heard anything about the matter, and that Bolton had not been questioned about the St Valentine's Day massacre.

Mr Ladd advised me that the Chicago papers quoted him as saying that we had no statement, oral or written, from Bolton concerning the massacre case, which was the statement he, Mr Ladd, had made to the papers.

I inquired if Bolton had been questioned concerning the massacre and Mr Ladd said that he was not questioned directly because they were anxious to get other information from him; that he was only asked if he knew anything about it and he replied that he did not, that he had nothing to do with it.

I remarked that the thing which had been causing me concern for some time was the thought that there might be a "leak" somewhere in the Chicago office; that I had this morning received some very reliable information, however, that the *Chicago American* has seven wire tappers who are tapping telephone wires; and that the *Chicago American* had had our wires tapped. I suggested to Mr Ladd that he check on this angle immediately through some man in the Chicago office who was efficient along that line. Mr Ladd stated that Agent J. L. Madala was the only man who could handle the matter, but that he was out on an assignment with Mr Connolly at the present time; that, however, he could get the telephone company to check on it for us. I stated that he could have the telephone company check on it first, and when Mr Madala returned he was to recheck on it.

Mr Ladd stated that he did not think that anyone in the Chicago office was "talking" or giving out information. I suggested that it might be a good idea to test the employees of the Chicago office by "planting" them with a fake story. Mr Ladd advised that he had done just that thing the other day, before the escape of Karpis and Campbell from Atlantic City, New Jersey; that he had one of the agents circulate a story concerning Karpis, and this story received wide circulation in the office; but that when the real story about Karpis came out, his fake story was, of course, stopped. Mr Ladd stated that he would give it another test along this same line.

I told Mr Ladd to keep me informed as to the results, and I suggested that the story be started that we had "someone" in custody.

I stated that if we caught the *Chicago American* wire tappers tapping our wires, it was my intention to prosecute them.

JOHN EDGAR HOOVER
Director
Division of Investigation
US Department of Justice
Washington DC

Memorandum for the Director

3.05 pm

I called Mr Nathan in connection with the stories in the press concerning the St Valentine's Day massacre, in which statements are made to the effect that "Assistant Director Harold Nathan gave the massacre story a left-hand confirmation", and asked just what he had said to the newspapers about this. Mr Nathan stated that the inquiries from the press came immediately after the break* and that he,

---

*After the story had made the news.

Nathan, had advised that "if he had ever made any such confession, I know nothing about it". I advised that the Director had issued a denial that any such statement was given and wants to emphasise that denial and the fact that nothing more should be said about the St Valentine's Day massacre. Mr Nathan further advised that the above quoted remarks constituted his first statement, but that later on, after talking with Ladd, he subsequently denied it.

E.A. TAMM
Division of Investigation
US Department of Justice
Washington DC

FBI Correspondence, January 25, 1935

Memorandum for the Director

11:50 am

While talking with Mr Ladd he advised that, in response to your call yesterday, he had the telephone company check the office lines, and had been advised that there were no taps on them and no sign of a tap, the dust being still on the wires and there being no signs that it has been disturbed.

Mr Ladd stated that he is going to start circulating a story there when the first opportunity arises.

E.A. TAMM
Division of Investigation
US Department of Justice
Washington DC

Memorandum for the Director

With reference to your memorandum of January 24, addressed to me concerning a telephonic conversation with Mr Ladd, relating to the possibility that the *Chicago American* has tapped the telephone wires of the Chicago Division office, I believe it would be advisable to avoid any reference to any completed action or suspicion of a telephone tap in talking with the Chicago office, since this procedure will undoubtedly put the newspaper on notice if the telephones are tapped. It is probable that if they tap one of the telephones, they have tapped them all, since most of the information to which they have apparent access, if obtained as a result of a telephone tap, is discussed on the confidential telephones. I believe it might be advisable when discussing this situation with anyone in the Chicago office to have them go outside of the Chicago office and call the Division from a pay station.

In this regard, we might discuss with the Chicago office for a period of several days by telephone the apprehension of Alvin Karpis, making it appear that he is actually in custody and of course if there were any leak then, the source of the information would be obvious.

E. A. TAMM
Division of Investigation
US Department of Justice
Washington DC

PUBLIC ENEMY ARRESTED

[*Chicago Evening American*, January 26, 1935]

POLICE SEIZE CLAUDE MADDOX

Gangster accused in massacre held for show-up

Claude Maddox, recently named as one of the gunmen in the St Valentine Day massacre, was locked up today at the detective bureau.

Maddox, who once led the notorious "Circus Gang", was involved in the slaughter by Byron

Bolton, whose confession of also taking part in the crime was printed exclusively by the *Chicago American*.

Maddox, a public enemy of long standing, was seized by two policemen as he drove up to his home at 2440 S. Oak Park Avenue in Berwyn early today.

The reported confession of Bolton, which was made to the government before he was sent to St Paul for a kidnapping trial, has not been turned over to police and without this evidence Chief of Detectives Sullivan said that Maddox could not be prosecuted. He will be held for the crime show-up tomorrow.

[*Chicago American*, January 26, 1935]

LAST OF GANG CAPTURED FOR MASSACRE

Gunman, unarmed, is corralled at home by Berwyn officers

Claude Maddox, gangster, gunman and public enemy, was seized and jailed today for investigation of his alleged part in the St Valentine's Day massacre.

Byron Bolton named Maddox as one of the machine gunners in an exclusive story printed by the *Chicago American*.

Maddox is the only one of the machine gunners named by Bolton who was alive or at large. He
was captured without sensation as he drove up in
front of his home at 2440 S. Oak Park Avenue,
Berwyn, at 5.30 am today by two policemen of the
suburb.

Detective Charles Rudderman and Patrolman
Frank Mitchell saw him drive past in an expensive
sedan and fell in behind. They trailed him to the
front door of his residence and as Maddox left his car
they placed him under arrest. A search disclosed that
he was unarmed, nor was there a gun in the car. He
was bustled off to the Berwyn police station despite
profane protests. The detective bureau in Chicago
was notified. Guarded by several officers, he was
then sped to the Chicago police headquarters and
taken to the bureau of identification.

When first seized he tried to escape arrest by
asserting that his name was John Moore, an old
alias. The two suburban policemen knew him,
however. As soon as his fingerprints were taken at
the bureau of identification he admitted his true
identity. Surlily, he refused to answer questions of
Deputy Chief of Detectives Walter Storms, who at
once notified Chief John L. Sullivan of the arrest.

[*Chicago American*]

BUTLER DEEMS BOLTON STORY TRUE PICTURE

That Byron Bolton's story of the St Valentine Day massacre appears to be a true picture of what actually took place was the opinion expressed today by Walker Butler, who as Assistant State's Attorney was in charge of the massacre investigation in 1929.

The most significant phase of Bolton's story, he said, was the description of Burke, Goetz and Winkler. Butler expressed the opinion that the presence of Murray Humphreys "might be wrong," and that if he had named Tony Capezio in his place the confession would be perfect. He said:

> We raided Bolton's home downstate after we trailed a trunk shipped from Capone's flat in Cicero. We missed Burke by just a few minutes. However, we found numerous pictures of Capone and others of his "mob". There was a picture of Burke in the Bolton home with two front teeth missing, and the witnesses to the slaying stressed the fact that one of the killers in police uniform had two front teeth missing.

Butler was associated in the investigation with Harry S. Ditchburne, also an Assistant State's Attorney, who also declared that Bolton's confession was supported by the facts gleaned at the time.

Sergt Samuel Loftus, a veteran of the police force, was the first policeman to enter the garage after the slaying of the seven. Today he said of Bolton's story:

> Every detail that Bolton outlined is true to my personal knowledge. I lived that case and as a matter of fact I am still working on it.

And Capt. Daniel Gilbert, who was then in charge of the police district where the murders took place and now in charge of the State's Attorney's police force, corroborated Sergt Loftus. He said:

> Bolton entered into the picture then as a likely bird. The Maddox angle is not only possible but I believe that it is the answer to the puzzle of his alibi. We knew Maddox was there, but couldn't prove it.

[*Chicago Herald and Examiner*, January 27, 1935]

MADDOX HELD ON SUSPICION

Claude Maddox, ex-Capone gangster, whom Byron Bolton is said to have named last week as one of the six participants in the St Valentine Day's massacre of 1929, was held at the detective bureau last night.

Two Berwyn policemen had arrested him as he entered his home at 2440 S. Oak Park Avenue. Turned over to Chicago police he was questioned by Detective Chief Sullivan. He scoffed at the massacre charge, but was held for today's show-up. The chief said he was "not wanted" here.

However, because of the persistent reports that federal agents really did get a confession from Bolton, there was belief in some quarters that Chief Sullivan's indifference was feigned and that Maddox would be kept under surveillance.

He has been running a saloon in Cicero since repeal melted the profits of illicit liquor. Bolton, arrested here by federal agents, is in St Paul, charged with the $200,000 Bremer kidnapping.

[*St Paul Dispatch*, January 26, 1935]

ALLEGED MASSACRE PRINCIPAL SEIZED

Chicago, Jan. 26 (AP). Claude Maddox, recently reported named in a confession by Byron Bolton as one of six men involved in the St Valentine's Day massacre of 1929, was seized early today by squads from the detective bureau at his home in suburban Berwyn.

He was taken to central police headquarters for questioning by John L. Sullivan, Chief of Detectives.

Now 35 years old, Maddox was former owner of the Circus Café where the gangsters were said to have consorted.

The massacre was said to have been attributed by Bolton to warfare between the Capone and Moran mobs over the profits of a dog racetrack at Lyons, Illinois. Federal officials promptly denied that Bolton had confessed or that he had been questioned concerning the massacre. Sullivan asserted, however, the Chicago police did not want Maddox. He indicated Maddox would be held for the regular Sunday show-up of crime suspects.

Maddox rose to prominence as a protégé of Al Capone. After the massacre he was arrested and quizzed, but released for lack of evidence. Later he was indicted for assault to kill but was not brought to trial. He still is listed as a public enemy by the Chicago Crime commission.

Harry Ditchburne, former Assistant State's Attorney who conducted the investigation into the massacre, disclosed today that when investigators from the homicide squad rushed from headquarters in the central police station to answer the massacre call they rode down the same elevator with Maddox, who had appeared in court on a disorderly conduct charge, and his attorney.

Maddox turned to his attorney and said, "Well that's one rap they can't hang on me," it was related by Ditchburne.

FBI Correspondence, January 26, 1935

Memorandum for the Director

10.40 am

I called Mr Connelley at Chicago in connection with the possibility that the *Chicago American* has a tap on the Chicago office telephone, and suggested that whenever anything of a confidential nature was to be furnished to Washington it would be well to go outside and call.

I suggested that it might be well to make some startling announcement over the telephone, such as stating that they have Karpis in custody, in order to see if the *Chicago American* gets it; that, although the telephone company had informed the division to the effect that no taps were being maintained, information had also reached the division to the effect that they have five or seven tapping telephones all the time. I requested advice as to the possibility of making it all look, particularly in connection with the stenographers and clerks, as though Perkins was Karpis, advising that the only worry in this connection would be that if we did get Karpis we would not know how to say over the telephone that it was genuine. Mr Connelley suggested that we could use the expression "Karpis K7" meaning that the conversation was "phoney". I advised that this would be fine, and suggested that we should talk about him over the telephone as though he were there, for the next day or so, and Connelley stated that he would do this.

Connelley further advised that they also have Fish Johnson, Dillinger's contact, up there too.

I cautioned Connelley against letting the agents on routine assignment, and the stenographers and clerical personnel, know just who they have in custody, advising that we would understand that when he says "Karpis K7", it would be "phoney".

E.A. TAMM
Division of Investigation
US Department of Justice
Washington DC

[*Chicago Daily Times*, January 26, 1935]

MADDOX IN CELL; NOBODY WANTS TO QUIZ HIM

Police and federal men both say they're "not interested"

Claude Maddox, alias Johnny Moore, found himself in a police cell today because someone said that he was one of the Capone machine gunners who wiped out seven Moran gangsters in the St Valentine Day massacre five years ago.

Chief of Detectives John L. Sullivan didn't quite know what to do about Maddox:

So far as I know Maddox has no connection with the massacre. We don't want him in Chicago for any crime. But on general principles we'll hold him for the show-up tomorrow afternoon.

Mr Maddox sat in his cell and brooded over the evils that can befall a poor, hardworking tavern-keeper who gets his name in the paper. Since the government repealed the "Scarface Al" Capone gang and prohibition, Maddox has been operating a tavern at 2241 South Cicero Avenue, Cicero. Maddox used to be a trusted member of the Capone gang, doing various odd jobs in the way of educating rivals to the wisdom of staying out the syndicate's territory.

Earlier this week reports were published that Byron Bolton, a Barker-Karpis gangster, had "confessed", naming himself, Maddox and four others as the machine gunners in the massacre. The only discrepancies in the report were that government agents who had Bolton in custody branded it as so much hooey and that Maddox—who is not one of the Dionne quintuplets*—was in court at the time of the massacre.

A reporter for the *Daily News* went out to see Maddox the day the "confession" was published. Maddox was found hiding behind a straightup

---

* Famous quintuplets, the first to have survived infancy, born in 1934 in Canada.

[pallet] of beer. He pointed out that he was in court at the time the massacre was perpetrated, that he couldn't be in two places at once and so had nothing to fear. The court statement was supported by his attorney, Tyrell Richardson, and by the officials.

Two zealous Berwyn policemen this morning seized Maddox as he was entering his home at 2440 South Oak Park Avenue. They found no weapons other than a nail file in his possession.

Berwyn authorities turned him over to Chicago police. After the show-up tomorrow Chief Sullivan said he would turn Maddox back to Berwyn. Daniel M. Ladd, agent in charge of the division of investigation here, said he didn't want Maddox.

Nobody wants Maddox, it seems, except his bartenders and waitress. And, so far as Chief Sullivan is concerned, they can have him and good riddance.

[*Washington Herald*]

POLICE PRESSING "MASSACRE" PROBE

Chicago, Jan. 27 (International News Service). Federal authorities were piling up corroborating evidence today to substantiate the story on the St Valentine's Day massacre told by Byron Bolton.

Although not enough evidence has been collected thus far to make a case against the surviving members of the gang responsible for the massacre, police believe that they soon will be in a position to destroy the entire mob.

[*Chicago Tribune*, January 27, 1935]

HELD FOR SHOW-UP

The alibi given by Claude Maddox when he was arrested after the 1929 St Valentine's Day massacre, that he was in court at the time the seven Moran gangsters were slain in the North Clark Street garage, was apparently regarded by the police as a bar to prosecution in the case yesterday when Chief of Detectives, John L. Sullivan, announced that Maddox would be held for the regular Sunday show-up "like any other hoodlum", but that he is not wanted for any particular crime. Federal authorities told Chief Sullivan they were not interested in the prisoner.

Maddox was seized by two Berwyn policemen yesterday morning as he was entering his home in that suburb, where he lived under the name of John Moore. He was turned over to the Chicago police.

[*Chicago Herald and Examiner*]

ST VALENTINE MASSACRE CONFESSED BY BOLTON FOR REVENGE ON CAPONE GANG

Accuses Al's aids of tipoff in Bremer case

Betrayed in the Bremer kidnapping by Al Capone's followers, one of "Scarface Al's" executioners in the St Valentine's Day massacre avenged himself and his comrades by laying the seven victims at Capone's door.

This was the explanation that came yesterday from police and government sources for the purported confession of Byron Bolton, naming Capone as instigator of the massacre, and himself, Fred Burke, Fred Goetz, Claude Maddox, Gus Winkler and Murray Humphreys as the slayers.

At St Paul, where they are under indictment with twenty others for the $200,000 ransom abduction of Edward G. Bremer, banker, Bolton and his associate, Arthur ("Doc") Barker, both were reported to be adding freely to the government's stock of information on the massacre and other crimes.

This information has not been relayed to state officials. As a consequence, Maddox, seized here Saturday after being named by Bolton, was released by Chicago police last night, since his part in the six-year-old crime remains to be substantiated. Bolton is understood to have revealed that the gang led by Burke was organised at least two years prior to the massacre, and that by 1928 he was a full-fledged member, driving the getaway car for the gunmen in a number of "jobs".

With Burke, Goetz, Winkler and himself in the gang were Joseph O'Riordan, once a member of the Detroit Purple gang, suspected in plot to kidnap Edsel Ford for $1,000,000 ransom in 1927, and Robert Conroy, brother-in-law of O'Riordan, a murderer, counterfeiter and the man whom Al Capone, at least, believed to be the Lindbergh kidnapper*.

Bolton's story is said to have revealed that the massacre was only one episode in the operations of the ruthless band.

He is reported to have asserted that Burke was the slayer of George Ziertara, a policeman killed at Toledo in 1928 when the gang captured an American Express money wagon containing $180,000 for the payroll of an auto plant.

* Famous baby kidnap case of 1932.

[*Associated Press*]

POLICE TO RELEASE ACCUSED GANGSTER

Chicago, Jan. 28. No one it seems wants Claude Maddox, one-time gangster named in an alleged "confession" in connection with the St Valentine's Day massacre, so Chicago police have turned him over to the suburban Berwyn police who arrested him. They will likely release him.

In the show-up here Maddox was not identified in any recent crimes. Local authorities said they were not able to connect him with the massacre because at the time of the killing he had an alibi that he was being arraigned in court on a disorderly conduct charge.

Federal authorities repeatedly have denied existence of the "Bolton confession". The *Herald and Examiner* nevertheless published a story yesterday again emphasising that the "confession" was a fact, and added that the reason Bolton talked was because he learned that followers of Al Capone reputedly had given government men information that led to unravelling of the Bremer case.

Federal agents also denied that story.

FURTHER DEVELOPMENTS

FBI Correspondence, February 1935

To J. Edgar Hoover, Justice Dept, Washington DC

February 2, 1935

Dear Sir,

Will you kindly forward to me as quickly as possible a complete description of all known gangsters in the St Valentine's Day massacre in Chicago, Illinois in 1929.

JAY SMITH
Capt. of Traffic, Tucson, Arizona

To Chief of Police, Tucson, Arizona—Attn Captain Jay Smith

February 11, 1935

My Dear Chief,

I have received your letter of February 2, 1935, in which you request a complete description of all of the known gangsters involved in the St Valentine's Day massacre in Chicago, Illinois.

You are advised that the files of this Division contain no information indicating the identity of the perpetrators of this offence. I know that newspaper dispatches have recently indicated that a subject of a Division investigation taken into custody at Chicago, Illinois had made a statement naming the perpetrators of this crime, but such dispatches were absolutely false and without foundation in fact.

I regret that I was unable to furnish you with any information of value in this matter.

JOHN EDGAR HOOVER
Director
Division of Investigation
US Department of Justice
Washington DC

To Mr J. E. Hoover, Chief of Federal Agents,
Washington DC

February 10, 1935

Dear Sir,

Now that the federal authorities have all the information leading up to the killers of the St Valentine's
massacre, what action is going to be taken to mete
out Justice?

Oh, I suppose there might be a technicality,
simply for the reason that what is left of the rats are
now serving prison terms, and maybe poor John
Law can't get in to prosecute until after their time
has been served. But this is where the law should
be revised "an eye for an eye", and these hardened
killers made to pay for their crimes strictly in
accordance with the original interpretation of the
law.

What is going to be done about it? If this case
is no longer in your hands, please pass this request
for justice along to the proper department, and
oblige.

"SLUMBERING PUBLIC INDIGNATION"
Chicago, Illinois

(Copy to: the President of the United States;
Chicago Herald and Examiner)

To Mr D.M. Ladd, FBI Chicago

Personal and Confidential

February 13, 1935

Dear Sir,

With further reference to my desire to ascertain the source of information obtained by Chicago papers, concerning official Bureau activities, prior to the time that any notice is given to the press, your attention is invited to the following facts which have been brought to my attention by Assistant Director Nathan.

Mr Nathan recalls that on the morning following the apprehension of Doc Barker, a newspaper reporter appeared at the Chicago Bureau office, and asked Mr Nathan whether it was not a fact that Alvin Karpis was in custody. You will recall that it was a belief of the Bureau, following the apprehension of Doc Barker, that the person who had been apprehended was Alvin Karpis, and accordingly, several long distance telephone calls were made between the Bureau and the Chicago office, pertaining to the apprehension of Karpis. While it is possible that the newspaper reporter who contacted Mr Nathan may have been merely guessing, these facts may have some significance in indicating that a telephone tap is or was being maintained upon telephones of the Chicago Bureau office. Please give this matter appropriate consideration, in connection with your efforts to ascertain the source of the information reaching the newspapers.

A similar letter is being addressed to Mr E.J. Connelley.

JOHN EDGAR HOOVER
Director
Federal Bureau of Investigation
US Department of Justice
Washington DC

[*Washington Star*]

ST VALENTINE'S DAY MASSACRE, GANGDOM'S WORST, UNSOLVED

Chicago marks sixth anniversary of crime that climaxed warfare between rival whisky barons

Chicago, Feb. 14. The rattle of machine guns dealing mass death echoed in the memories of Chicagoans today as they noted the sixth anniversary of the crime which left the blackest smudge on the city's crime-encrusted face—the still unsolved St Valentine's Day massacre of 1929.

It was this slaughter of seven men which, more than any other single crime, gave Chicago a reputation as a city of gangsters and sudden death. It climaxed the gang wars between underworld factions, then narrowed down to a battle between the forces of Al Capone and George (Bugs) Moran.

The mystery of the St Valentine's Day massacre appeared near a solution for a time last month, when it was reported that Byron Bolton, Bremer kidnapping suspect, had confessed and named five underworld characters as his associates in the killing.

The reported solution, however, was greatly discounted when Claude Maddox, named in the supposed confession, was arrested and promptly released, with the explanation that police had nothing on him.

Chicago was gay with hearts and flowers on February 14, 1929. All seemed quiet at 2122 North Clark Street, the garage that was the headquarters of the Moran gang. There bootleg whisky was brought in, "cut" and prepared for delivery.

Moran and Terry Druggan, West Side public enemy, had just left the garage when two men in police uniforms drove up. The two men forced their way into the garage.

"Line up," they commanded curtly.

The seven men inside, thinking it was a routine raid, lined up against the wall. A moment later several other men entered. There was a roar of machine gun shots. Six riddled bodies fell to the ground. A seventh victim lived only a few hours. He died in hospital without recovering sufficiently to name assailants. That was the St Valentine's Day massacre that was the beginning of the end of gangdom in Chicago.

[*New York Journal*]

FINGER POINTS AT MASTER GANGSTER

It's hardly more than a knowing whisper so far. The G-men don't admit it. They never do. But, persistently, the word has run the course up and down Chicago's police and underworld "grapevines" until finally it has penetrated prison walls and reached the ears of a short, swarthy, saturnine man—the most notorious character of our times—as he paces his cell on lonely Alcatraz Island, off the western coast.

And its awful purport has been something to torment his waking hours and by night his dreams. The word is that they're dusting off the electric chair for Al Capone.

The G-men have got him, several Chicago police officials believe, got him at last and got him right. Not for income tax evasion and contempt of court, the rap for which he is doing 11 years at Alcatraz. That's mere trivia in the code of criminal justice. This charge may be murder, pitiless mass murder; brought back to Chicago after all these years, the Chicago police allege, by the confession of one of his ex-triggermen.

The confession, if it's all the underworld faces and the police believe, exhumes in all its ghastly gory horror the St Valentine massacre of the "Bugs" Moran mob on February 14, 1929.

Seven men against a wall. A volley of machine-gun fire. Seven men on the ground, inert, lifeless, shot through the back as they stood facing the wall, their hands raised. For six years, the slaughter has been just a police record, "unsolved", all but forgotten.

But now, unless the tip has been strangely garbled, Byron Bolton, one of Al's better "guns" in the olden, golden days, has pointed the finger at his old pals and friends—and Al was undoubtedly one of these. Byron, they say, has even admitted that he was one of the actual slaughterers that fine, sanguinary day in a little garage at 2122 North Clark Street, Chicago.

The others, according to this alleged feature confession, were: Humphreys, successor to Capone after Al was "unavoidably detained out of town"; Fred "Killer" Burke, one of the real desperadoes; Gus Winkler, North Side gambling boss; Claude Maddox, former head of the now obsolete Circus Gang; Fred Goetz, who claimed to be a graduate of the University of Illinois.

It is generally believed that if the case looks strong enough, it will bring Humphreys back from Leavenworth to stand trial and at the same time, make every effort to persuade Michigan to yield its claim upon Burke.

As for Capone, it has reason to know exactly where he is for 24 hours of every day. Some of his time recently has even been spent in solitary confinement.

But whatever the outcome, Chicago police officials seem practically unanimous in their confidence that reports of the Bolton confession are authentic. Says former Chief of Detectives William H. Shoemaker:

> It has all the earmarks of the truth. I have always
> believed that Maddox was in on the slaughter.
> Strength is given that idea by the fact that his car,
> which we believe was used for the get-away, was found
> burned and dismantled several days after the killings.

Says the present Chief of Detectives Sullivan:

> It sounds like the truth. It's the same dope that stool
> pigeons from the Capone gang brought us after the
> massacre. But we never could prove it. It shouldn't be
> hard to build up a murder case from that confession.

Captain Andrew Barry, of the Hudson Avenue station, adds that Humphreys was one he had always suspected in connection with the crime, while Captain John Stege declares that ballistic tests of guns found in Burke's possession when he was arrested in Michigan proved that they were used in the North Clark Street shambles.

Moreover, Chief Sullivan points out, Bolton was identified from his picture as "my nice young man roomer" in the words of the landlady of a boarding house across the street from the garage. Bolton, in his confession, is understood to have referred to his quarters as a lookout room.

Federal authorities deny possessing such a confession, of course. But for ten days it professed to discredit stories that it was holding Mrs Luther Gillis, wife of George "Baby Face" Nelson. At another time it refused to admit that it had Arthur "Doc" Barker for complicity in the $200,000 Bremer snatch.

And it is fact, not fancy, that Byron Bolton has done considerable talking since being collared January 10 last in connection with this Bremer case.

At first the old Capone mob was sceptical about reports that Bolton was spilling all he knew, their reaction being more forceful than elegant: "Bunk! Byron's a stand-up guy. He ain't singing."

But later, when he took the stand and turned state's evidence in the Bremer case, they had to admit that Byron was a "canary" after all, that he had sung in G-flat for the G-man in St Paul.

The only question that remains is: how far did Byron go with his vocal lessons? Did he sing right through his repertoire or did he just acknowledge a few request numbers? Undoubtedly a lot of people would like to know and one of them may be Capone.

In any case, the Chicago police declare that the extermination of the "Bugs" Moran mob was something to which Capone could not have been totally indifferent. Moran was cleaning up with his North Side "trade" during prohibition and had resisted all attempts to muscle in. He probably was expecting trouble but not the showdown that was so diabolically arranged.

They waited until the following list were in the garage:

Pete Gusenberg and Tim Boyer, ex-convicts; Pete's brother, Frank; James Clark, brother-in-law of Moran; John May, garage mechanic; Al Weinshank, speakeasy owner; and Dr R.H. Schwimmer, who liked to play around with the tough guys for the thrill of it. He would have his last great thrill this time.

In the doorway stood two men with guns, said in the purported confession of Bolton to have been Burke and Goetz. They were dressed as Chicago policemen, and at a word from them, the assemblage obediently raised its hands and marched over to face the opposing wall. Then in marched other killers and mowed them down where they stood.

It probably seemed a good idea at the time. But was it?

FBI Correspondence, April 1935–September 1936

To Director, FBI, Washington DC

Personal and confidential

April 6, 1935

Dear Sir,

Reference is made to Bureau letters of February 13 and March 30, 1935, referring to the source of the information upon which certain newspaper articles were based, and possibly indicating that this information as to Bureau activities had been furnished to the press by someone at Chicago.

I have given this matter considerable thought and attention as well as making certain discrete inquiry, and also by making what I believe were tests, inferences which might lead to someone giving out this information, provided it was anyone connected with the Chicago office, and in my opinion it is very doubtful that anybody at the Chicago office is intentionally furnishing any information which might reach the newspapers.

In most of the instances where stories have appeared, while we have no definite information indicating the source of these, it is apparent that the information indicated could very well have been obtained from other sources or circumstances than a contact with somebody associated with the office. The only matter which seems to be impossible of satisfactory explanation is the information which was given out as to the fact that Arthur Barker was held at the Chicago office, as to which it is noted that several days after he was held, the newspapers made inquiry and obtained copies of his identification order, and it is possible that they may have exhibited his picture in the neighborhood in which the raids were conducted on the night of January 8, 1935, resulting in an identification to them by some person who knew of him having been apprehended on the night of January 8, or at least knew of him having been a resident of 432 Surf Street, or a visitor at 3820 Pine Grove Avenue, Chicago.

The references as to Helen Gillis having been held at the Chicago office, particularly when she was first apprehended and held there, it is believed are known to the Bureau, that is, as to the source from which the newspapers obtained the information indicated.

As to the articles which appeared the night before Helen Gillis appeared before the Grand Jury in January 1935, no one was aware of the fact that she was held here at the time until late the day before she appeared before the Grand Jury, at which time this information was furnished to the United States Attorney at Chicago, Illinois, and it is possible that the US Attorney made some reference to the fact that he intended to use her before the Grand Jury, and this may have been the source from which the newspapers inferred that she was being held by us at that time. It is known definitely that it was announced early the following morning that she would appear before the Grand Jury that morning to testify in that case, as this was announced to the newspapers by the US Attorney.

The article which appeared as to the alleged confession of William Byron Bolton and his connection with the St Valentine's Day massacre February 14, 1929, was based entirely upon misinformation, inasmuch as he had made no such statement to anyone, and at the time these articles appeared Bolton had been taken to St Paul and surrendered for official custody at that place, indicating of course definitely that we previously had had him in custody. The recent articles appearing in the papers referring to the alleged confession furnished by Jess Doyle to federal agents at Kansas City I do not believe had any reference to any information obtained at Chicago, and judging from the report from the Kansas City office that the Associated Press dispatches there do not show a dispatch to St Paul, and the explanation offered by the representative of the Associated Press at St Paul that he had received this in an Associated Press dispatch from Kansas City, this would indicate that the source of this information was probably St Paul, and while I have no information upon which to base same, it is my belief that possibly Attorney DeCourcey at that point may be responsible for this article which appeared.

Previously we have had a very careful check made of the telephones at the Chicago office, and the telephone company has indicated there is no possibility of a tap on our lines here, and also judging by the conversations which have been had over these lines, and the information transmitted, it is my belief that the papers did not have this source of information, because of the fact that many more important things have been discussed, which could very easily have been the subject matter of press releases if they had been able to overhear such conversations.

E.J. CONNELLEY
Special Agent in Charge
FBI Chicago

Memorandum for Mr Tamm

3.51 pm, June 13, 1935

Re: Byron Bolton

Mr Waldrop telephoned and stated that a report was being carried in the *Chicago Herald and Examiner* to the effect that Byron Bolton had made a complete confession. I advised Mr Waldrop that this report was not true; that Bolton was taken into custody by the Bureau and tried and convicted for his part in the Bremer case, but that the reports that he had made a confession clearing up the St

Valentine's Day massacre at Chicago were unfounded.

JOHN EDGAR HOOVER
Director FBI
Washington DC

*Memorandum for Joseph B. Keenan, Acting
Attorney General*

August 27, 1936

With reference to your inquiry as to information furnished by Byron Bolton concerning the St Valentine's Day massacre in Chicago, Illinois in 1929, you are advised that Bolton was questioned concerning this offence. Bolton stated that the persons who actually perpetrated this massacre were Fred Goetz, Gus Winkler, Fred Burke, Ray Nugent and Bob Carey. Bolton stated that he personally purchased the Cadillac touring car that was used in this massacre, having been furnished with the money to make this purchase by Louis Lipschultz. Bolton claims that he purchased this car from the Cadillac Company on Michigan Avenue in Chicago sometime before the massacre happened and assumed at the time that he purchased the car that it was to be used in hauling alcohol. Bolton believes that he used the name James Martin in purchasing the car. The object of this massacre, according to Bolton, which was planned by members of the Capone organisation, was for the purpose of eliminating "Bugs" Moran from the bootlegging racket in Chicago. Bolton claims that the plot to perpetrate this killing was initially developed at a place on Cranberry Lake, six miles north of Couderay, Wisconsin. Al Capone, Gus Winkler, George Ziegler, Louis Campagna, Fred Burke, Bill Pacelli (reported to be an Illinois State Senator) and Dan Saratella are reported to have been at the resort operated by George on Cranberry Lake at the time the killing was first planned, this being in October or November of 1928. Bolton states that Jimmy McCrussen and Jimmy "The Swede" Moran were selected to watch "Bugs" Moran's garage, since they both knew Moran by sight, in order to learn his movements. Bolton states that Al Capone went to Florida before the massacre was perpetrated and left Frank Mitti in charge of the operations and that one Frankie Reo, now dead, was Mitti's assistant in the transaction. Bolton claims that none of the actual perpetrators wore police uniforms, although they did wear police badges and that when the killing took place the persons actually perpetrating therein did not know the identity of each of their victims but rather than risk the possibility of missing Moran, killed all the persons found in the garage.

As indicated above, Bolton states that Fred Goetz, Gus Winkler, Fred Burke, Ray Nugent and Bob Carey were the actual perpetrators of the massacre. According to Bolton, Claude Maddox of St

Louis, Tony Capesia of Chicago and a man known as "Shocker" also of St Louis, burned the Cadillac car after the massacre.

Bolton has consistently denied that he personally participated in the massacre and has expressed a willingness to confront any one of the individuals named by him, accusing him of participation in this offence.

In discussing this matter, Bolton has informed Special Agents of this Bureau that at the time of the St Valentine's Day massacre, Chief of Detectives Stege of the Chicago Police Dept was on the payroll of the Capone syndicate, receiving $5,000 per week, and kept the members of the syndicate informed as to the whereabouts of Bugs Moran.

JOHN EDGAR HOOVER
Director FBI
Washington DC

*Memorandum for the Assistant to Attorney
General, Mr Joseph Keenan*

September 15, 1936

With reference to the request made of you some weeks ago by State's Attorney Courteney of Chicago for information in the possession of the FBI concerning the persons responsible for the St Valentine's massacre in Chicago on February 14, 1929, you will recall that I informed you that Byron Bolton had furnished us certain information relative to this matter. In discussing this matter with you, it was my understanding that you felt that this investigation should be conducted by the Bureau; that is to say, that we should proceed with the location of the various subjects who were involved in this massacre and when located and evidence gathered, then it would be time to determine the procedure to be taken relative to presenting it to State's Attorney Courteney.

My purpose in bringing this again to your attention is due to the fact that the federal statute penalising unlawful flight to avoid prosecution was dated May 14, 1934, whereas the crime was committed, of course, on February 14, 1929. In memorandum received from the department under date of June 25, 1934, the FBI was instructed that the Departmental interpretation was that this statute did not apply to past transactions but covers only actions which have been in violation of this law after it became effective. Consequently, I would appreciate being advised as to whether, in view of this interpretation, it is still believed desirable for the Bureau to proceed with an investigation of this matter. The Bureau has no objection to conducting this investigation, but my only doubt is as to our jurisdiction.

JOHN EDGAR HOOVER
Director FBI
Washington DC

Memorandum for the Director

9.21 am, September 19, 1936

Mr Holtzoff telephoned me and asked, "Just what was the St Valentine's Day massacre?" I outlined to Mr Holtzoff briefly what took place in this matter, and told him that it was just an outbreak of gang warfare in Chicago.

He then wanted to know if the Bureau thought there was any federal violation involved in this matter. I told him that we can see absolutely no federal violation in this situation; that while Mr Keenan was in the Criminal Division, we received a memorandum from him stating that no offence would come within the provisions of the unlawful flight statute which was committed prior to the time of its enactment for the reason that otherwise, you would have an *ex post facto* [after the fact] law.

E.A. TAMM
FBI
Washington DC

Memorandum for the Director

September 21, 1936

With reference to our conversation recently concerning the St Valentine's Day massacre, I desire to advise you that the report of Agent Brennan dated at St Paul, Minnesota, July 24, 1935 in the Bremer kidnapping case was received in the Bureau on July

27. At that time, Mr Newby was supervising this case and the fact that Bolton had furnished the details of the massacre was not brought to my attention. Although Mr Newby addressed a memorandum to you on August 3, 1935, containing an excerpt upon another situation from this report of Agent Brennan's, no reference was made to Bolton's statement concerning the massacre. The weekly summary report of Agent Newby summarising the developments in this case makes no reference to Bolton's statement in this regard.

E.A. TAMM
FBI
Washington DC

[*Chicago Daily News*, December 31, 1936]

CONVICT BARES STORY OF
VALENTINE MASSACRE

A new and revised version of the Clark Street carnage of St Valentine's Day seven years ago is in the hands of Chicago police officials. Police officials, however, maintained a close-mouthed silence and decline emphatically to discuss the report.

According to information supplied to the *Daily News*, the new light on the massacre of seven of George "Bugs" Moran's mobsters in a garage at 2212 Clark Street in the course of prohibition's eruptive era, came from Byron Bolton, now serving sentence in a federal penitentiary for confessed participation in the ransom abductions of Edward G. Bremer and William Hamm.

Bolton, it is reported, about four months ago, after his conviction and incarceration for the federal offence, made a statement which outlined the wholesale killing in detail. This information was recently turned over to Police Commissioner James P. Allman.

In the statement, it was said Bolton named the participants in the massacre. Some are known to be dead and one or two others are reported to be still alive. Whether he implicated himself in the statement could not be learned.

Police officials declared today "that they would like to talk to Bolton". Canvassed for confirmation of the reported statement, Chicago police officials asserted they could not discuss it. It was reported that the homicide squad, under the direction of Lieut. Otto Erlanson, is now checking the statements alleged to have been made by Bolton.

Chief of Detectives John L. Sullivan, in refusing to deny or verify the reported statement, said, "If it were a case of any other caliber I might be disposed to discuss it. I will not discuss this case under any consideration, however."

Bolton, 37 years old, a former sailor, has been identified at various times as a man sought by the Chicago police for participation in the St Valentine's Day massacre.

After the mass slaying, investigation revealed that two men had rented a room directly across the street from the grease-soaked death chamber a week before machine-gun executioners strode into the garage and mowed down its seven occupants. From this vantagepoint they mapped out the "lay of the land" for the murderers. In the abandoned room was found a letter addressed to "Byron Bolton" and it bore the postmark of Virden, Illinois.

Investigators went to Virden and found Bolton's parents living on a farm between it and Thayer, both small towns in the central part of the state. A picture obtained from Bolton's father was identified as that of one of the men who had rented the "death watch" room.

Bolton's movements were then traced to St Louis, where it was learned he had been a chauffeur for Fred "Killer" Burke, also variously identified as a participant in the massacre. Burke is now serving a life sentence in the Michigan penitentiary for another murder.

FBI Correspondence, October 1936– December 1938

Memorandum for Mr J. Edgar Hoover

October 12, 1936

This will acknowledge the receipt of your memorandum of September 15, 1936, with reference to the request of State's Attorney Courteney of Chicago for information in the possession of the Bureau concerning the persons responsible for the St Valentine massacre in Chicago on February 14, 1929.

It is noted that you call attention to this matter because of the fact that the federal statute penalising unlawful flight to avoid prosecution was dated May 14, 1934, and was approved May 18, whereas the crime in question was committed on February 14, 1929.

In this connection you are advised that although as indicated in the memorandum under date of June 23, 1934 addressed to you, the Departmental interpretation was that the statute did not apply to past transactions, but covers only actions which have been in violation of this law after it became effective, it may well be that in the circumstances presented in this case, the individuals responsible for perpetration of this crime might well have been in the state of Illinois and within its criminal jurisdiction on the date this statute was passed and may have moved from there sometime thereafter.

As a consequence, therefore, if they were in the state of Illinois after that date, and as they are still fugitives from justice in that state, if they subsequently left it for the purpose of avoiding prosecution to enter another state, territory, possession of the United States, the District of Columbia or any foreign country, they would be within the terms of the statute.

If such is the case, then there is no question but that the FBI would have investigative jurisdiction and you are so advised.

JOSEPH B. KEENAN
Assistant to the Attorney General
Department of Justice
Washington DC

To Mr E. J. Connelley, FBI Cleveland

October 27, 1936

Dear Mr Connelley,

I am attaching hereto a copy of a memorandum prepared in the Bureau under date of October 26, 1936 which summarises the information contained in the Bureau files concerning the identity of the perpetrators of the St Valentine's Day massacre. I desire that at the earliest possible date you personally call upon Commissioner Allman of the Chicago Police Dept and furnish a copy of this memorandum to him, explaining that this is all of the information developed during the Bureau's investigation into the facts surrounding the perpetration of the St Valentine's Day massacre.

Please advise me fully of the results of your interview with Commissioner Allman.

JOHN EDGAR HOOVER
Director FBI
Washington DC

Memorandum re: St Valentine's Day Massacre

October 26, 1936

During the course of the investigation in connection with the kidnapping of Edward George Bremer of St Paul, Minnesota, the FBI obtained certain information relative to those persons alleged to have been responsible for the perpetration of the St Valentine massacre at Chicago, Illinois on February 14, 1929.

Byron Bolton has furnished Special Agents with the information that the persons actually committing the murders in the garage on North Clark Street, Chicago, Illinois were Fred Goetz, alias George Zeigler, Gus Winkler, Fred Burke, Ray Nugent and Bob Carey, alias Conroy, and who also may have been known as Ted Newberry. Bolton has admitted that he purchased the Cadillac touring car used by the murderers in the perpetration of the massacre. He stated that the car was purchased by him from a Cadillac company located on Michigan Avenue in Chicago, Illinois, and he believes that he used the name of James Martin in purchasing this car. He stated that Louis Lipschultz gave him the money to purchase this car, and was taken to the place of purchase by Lipschultz. Bolton stated that at the time he purchased the car he assumed it was to be used in hauling alcohol.

Bolton stated that the purpose of the massacre was to eliminate "Bugs" Moran, who had a gang which was the rival of the so-called Al Capone syndicate. He advised that the plans for the massacre were formulated at a resort owned by Fred Goetz on Cranberry Lake, six miles north of Couderay, Wisconsin during October or November, 1928. He stated that the following persons were present at this resort at the time the plans were made to kill "Bugs" Moran: Al Capone, Gus Winkler, Fred Goetz, Louis Campagna, Fred Burke, Bill Pacelli, who later became an Illinois State Senator, and Dan Saratella. Bolton stated that he knows these persons were at the resort because Goetz came to him and requested that he, Bolton, take a load of spaghetti and foodstuffs to the resort, and that these parties remained on the place at Cranberry Lake for two or three weeks, and this information can be verified by Frank Crandall and Eddy Anderson, guides who took the various individuals named hunting and fishing, and who lived in the vicinity of the resort. Charles Allison was a caretaker of the resort at that time and could also verify the presence of these various persons at that place.

Bolton furnished the further information that Claude Maddox, alias Johnny Moore, formerly of St Louis, Missouri, Tony Capesio of Chicago, Illinois and a man known as "Shocker", who was also from St Louis, Missouri, burned the Cadillac car after the massacre.

Bolton denied that he participated in the massacre in any way and stated that the persons who occupied the apartment across the street from the garage at 2122 North Clark Street, watching for the appearance of "Bugs" Moran, were James Moran, alias "Jimmy the Swede" and Jimmy McCrussen; that the operations on the day of the massacre were carried on from Claude Maddox's Circus Café on the north side of Chicago. Bolton advised that Al Capone was in Miami, Florida on February 14, 1929, but that Frank Nitti took charge of things in Capone's absence, and that he was assisted by Frankie Reo, now dead. Bolton stated that none of the participants in the massacre wore police uniforms at the time the murders were committed, but that they did wear police badges.

Mrs Irene Stanley, née Irene Dorsey, Wilmington, Illinois, who lived with Fred Goetz several years prior to his death, advised Special Agents that in 1925 and 1926 Fred Goetz, Byron Bolton and Frankie Dias operated a still in Springfield, Illinois, and in 1927 they moved to Chicago, Illinois and joined the so-called Capone syndicate, being closely associated with Al Capone, Ralph Capone, Jack Gusik, Harry Gusik, Gus Winkler, Ted Newberry, Jack McGurn and Fred "Killer" Burke.

Irene Stanley stated to agents that it was her information that the actual killers in the St Valentine's Day massacre were Ted Newberry, Gus Winkler and Fred Goetz; that because the police learned that Bolton had rented the apartment which was used for lookout purposes across the street from the garage where the massacre took place, Bolton became a fugitive and began using the name O. B. Carter.

Mrs Gus Winkler, widow of Gus Winkler, states that in the latter part of January 1929, Gus Winkler brought Fred Goetz to her apartment in Chicago, Illinois, and a few days later Goetz again appeared at the apartment wearing a police uniform.

After the massacre Gus Winkler and Bob Carey were in the Winkler apartment and spent most of the afternoon sitting in front of the windows. From the discussions Mrs Winkler overheard between Carey, Winkler and Goetz, she learned that Bolton and Jimmy Moran had been assigned to watch the garage on North Clark Street for the appearance of the mob, and gave the signal to the killers when the gang entered the garage. She states that the murderers were staying in the home of Rocca de Croce, which was located nearby; that she later found bullet-proof vests and a police uniform in the closet of her apartment.

Upon being advised by Louis Campagna that he was suspected by the police of being implicated in the massacre, Gus Winkler fled from Chicago, Illinois, as did Fred Burke.

Seven members of "Bugs" Moran's mob were killed, but "Bugs" Moran did not put in his appearance at the garage on North Clark Street and therefore escaped assassination.

To Mr E.J. Connelley, FBI Cleveland

November 16, 1936

Dear Mr Connelley,

With reference to my communication of October 27, 1936, transmitting a memorandum pertaining to the perpetration of the St Valentine's Day massacre, I would appreciate being advised of the details of your conference with Commissioner Allman of the Chicago Police Department, as soon as you are able to arrange this conference.

JOHN EDGAR HOOVER
Director FBI
Washington DC

To Director FBI, Washington DC

December 29, 1938

Dear Sir,

As of possible information to the Bureau in connection with the St Valentine's Day massacre in Chicago, I am forwarding herewith copy of a memorandum submitted by Special Agent J. R. Green relative to information received by him from Simon Russel of Gary, Indiana.

D.M. LADD
Special Agent in Charge
FBI Chicago

Memorandum for Special Agent in charge
D. M. Ladd

December 23, 1938

Re: St Valentine Day massacre

On the late afternoon of December 20, 1938, Simon Russel, 830 West 11th Avenue, Gary, Indiana, furnished the following information to the Chicago field office:

He stated that he was employed at the Pyramid Engineering & Manufacturing Company, 1256 Wellington Avenue, which was under the management of Mike M. Kaufman, as a toolmaker; that he worked at this place for about a week in the month of February the year of the so-called St Valentine's Day massacre; then after being laid off about one week, he was called back to work the day of the massacre (St Valentine's Day).

About 9.30 or 10 am on that day three men came in one automobile to the shop and talked with Kaufman at his desk in the office, this being a small shop, and later about 30 men came to the shop, coming in several automobiles; that some of these latter men opened up a wooden box which they had brought with them, and took out an instrument, he seeing only a long tube, which he did not closely observe, and after taking it out covered it up with a black canvas so it looked like a camera when this machine was set up in the middle of the shop.

The first three men who had come in, had had revolvers when they came in, and after the others had set up the instant [mentioned earlier] machine, which he believed to be a machine gun, Kaufman gave a revolver to a part of these men after they had taken drinks given to them by Kaufman. T. Banke, 8105 Vincennes Avenue, was the leader of one group of these men who had come in automobiles, and he also gave revolvers to his bunch, the two groups being divided about equally; that shortly thereafter four more men came in an automobile, one of whom wore a policeman's uniform. He later stated that this man, who wore the policeman's uniform, was later identified as Dillinger. Alexander Laurenites, however, was the leader of this group of four, they also having revolvers. Thereupon one of the men from the Kaufman gang and another from Laurenites gang took the machine gun, which had been disguised as a camera, and placed it in one of the automobiles, whereupon all of the men left the shop. However, just before they left Kaufman asked him what this machine was, evidently in an effort to see how much he knew, and when Russel replied it looked like a camera Kaufman stated that they would take his picture when they came back.

He stated that he informed the other fellow employee, who had been left in the shop with him, by the name of Frederickson, what Kaufman had said relative to the taking of their picture when they returned, Frederickson suggested that Russel and he leave as "there would be hell to pay" when the crowd came back. Whereupon he and Frederickson left the shop and separated. Russel stopped in several saloons, where he got drinks, and it was late when he went to his room at 1417 49th Avenue, Cicero. The next morning he read in the papers of the St Valentine Day massacre at twelve or more blocks away from the Pyramid Engineering & Manufacturing Co.

The second day after this Kaufman phoned to him to come back to work, whereupon he worked at this place about one week or so. However, Kaufman never mentioned this incident to him until a year or so later, when Russel was looking for work. Kaufman asked him who did the massacre job, and he told Kaufman he didn't know. However, he was sure that Kaufman suspicioned [suspected] him, Russel, with knowing Kaufman had participated in the same. Russel further stated that when he came to work that St Valentine's Day morning Kaufman had given him something to drink that had left him dopey, and he believed he had given him this so that he would not fully realise or remember what was to take place later.

Russel stated that Mr and Mrs Joe Pasco, his sister and her husband, 553 Connecticut Street, Gary, Indiana, and their son Joe Jr, who lives with them and is married, suspected him with knowledge as to Kaufman's connection with the instant Valentine massacre. His brother-in-law, Joe Pasco, had been connected with Kaufman in various illegal activities before this, and at the present time, and that he was one of the gang, but was not present on instant occasion; that his sister and both the Sr and Jr Pasco have tried to get him so he could not tell this story or what he knew relative to instant massacre. He stated that on one occasion, when he had gone to a friend's house for the night, while he was asleep Joe Pasco Jr, his nephew, tried to get his friends, with whom he was staying, to let him go up to Russel's room so he could shoot him while he was sleeping. He also stated that John Grakey, 841 Virginia Street, Gary, Indiana and Stanley Meseveschs, 425 Adams, Gary, Indiana, were, with many other members of this gang, but these are the only persons whose names he knew.

Russel stated that he had just recently tried to tell this to the Gary, Indiana Police Dept, but as their administration was changing on the first of the year they were not interested. He insisted that the man appearing in the guise of a policeman on instant occasion, as heretofore described, was John Dillinger. He further stated that he understood this gang had been partly broken, but that Mike, George and Albert Kaufman, who were sons of Mike Kaufman, Sr, are members of this gang, still running at large, and that they have been making plates for the making of counterfeit money, which they had also made; that he had seen the plates. He stated that it was because of fear that members of this gang were trying to get him, and that this was the reason for making the complaint at the present time, which the writer remarked to him was rather a late time for him to furnish said information. He stated that for the past few years he has been engaged in the sharpening and taking care of dentists' tools, and that for the past five years or so he had ground the dental instruments for Dr George A. Matula, who has an office on the 27th floor of the Bankers Building. The telephone directory shows a George Matula at 105 West Adams Street, this building address, telephone State 3706.

While Mr Russel was hard to understand, yet he appeared rational, and the writer was unable to state whether he was mentally off.

The writer submitted these facts to Acting Special Agent in Charge E.J. Gebben, who started to place them in memorandum form, but that there was nothing in which this office at present was concerned in connection therewith, after which the writer suggested that Russel submit his information with reference to this gang making counterfeit plates to the Secret Service. He indicated that he would do so, and would probably also go to the Chicago Police Department.

J. R. GREEN
Special Agent

TENTH ANNIVERSARY
AND AFTER

[*Chicago Daily News*, February 14, 1939]

VALENTINE DAY AND CAPONE MOB
PROSPERS AGAIN

Veterans of massacre in right with machine,
so they celebrate

Ten years ago today Al Capone's executioners
reached an all-time high for gangster butchery in

the St Valentine's Day massacre in which seven men were stood against a wall and shot down as fast as a machine gun could spray their backs.

Today the Capone veterans of the Moran gang slaughter are on top again. In right with the Kelly-Nash machine, reputedly through organization of gambling privileges in cahoots with William Robert ("Billy") Skidmore, the Capone old guard is celebrating Valentine's Day as the best of good times.

A careful check covering several weeks reveals that the period ending with the mayoral primaries, February 28, is likely to be the most prosperous enjoyed by the mob, not excepting the fat years marked by the St Valentine's Day massacre.

Skidmore, agent for a long line of political pirates and described by State's Attorney Courteney as the "fixer" through whom Capone mobsters and other racketeers in many lines obtain protection, runs a scrap-iron business at 2840 South Kedzie Avenue. Latest reports reaching underworld circles describe Skidmore as "alarmed over the prospect of Courteney becoming the next mayor of Chicago".

The Capone gang has reorganized and widened its field. Concessions granted by the Kelly-Nash machine in return for support of Mayor Kelly at the polls on primary day have skyrocketed receipts. Skidmore, as go-between, conducted negotiations and brought them to a successful conclusion.

Capone "big shots", immune from interference under the present city administration, have taken over the clubhouse of a Chicago race track. Its elaborate offices are being used as their headquarters.

"Out there at this time of the year," said a noted law enforcement officer, "they are as well hidden as they would be if conducting their rackets from the superintendent's office of some graveyard."

A mysterious figure in the history of gangdom in Chicago has been brought to light by the survey. Paul Ricca, heretofore a handyman but recently promoted to "big shot" leadership, is now the acting top-notch boss of the mob Al Capone once led. Frank "The Enforcer" Nitti, who took over after Cousin Al had been tossed into prison for income-tax frauds, is said to have sponsored Ricca's rise to power.

Nitti, whose real name is Francesco Raffele Nitto, spends his winters in Florida. He makes frequent trips here, however. At the time of his last visit, said to have taken place in December, he occupied his Chicago apartment in Gladys Avenue, near Lotus Avenue. While in Chicago Nitti becomes "Frank Raddo".

Under the Ricca regime, Jack Guzik remains in charge of gambling operations. Rocco De Grazia has been assigned to supervision of numerous dens of vice located in Cook County but outside the city limits. The gang's Chicago brothels are to have a new operating head.

Comment around 22nd and State and 19th and Dearborn, where the gang operates two of the city's biggest vice dives, is that Ricca will fill the position this week.

Eddie "Dutch" Vogel continues as head of the slot machine department—a racket viewed generally as "pushed around a lot of late" but actually flourishing since Skidmore waved his magic wand over the City Hall.

Ralph "Bottles" Capone, brother of Al, stays on as assistant in charge of gambling spots and brothels in Cicero. One of the latter has 35 inmates.

Murray Humphries, alias John Humphreys, one of Ricca's chief aids under the new setup, takes over management of some of the mob's leading business enterprises, such as towel and linen supply service, sale of bottled waters to night clubs and saloons and numerous other lines. In addition, he will carry on the cleaning and dyeing racket the gang sponsors.

Louis "Little New York" Campagna, for years Nitti's bodyguard, has a brand new assignment. He cracks down on bookie joints, forcing the proprietors to agree to a cut. As a result, one third of the profits are turned over to the gang's representative, installed on the spot.

Lawrence "Dago Lawrence" Mangano does to night clubs exactly what "Little New York" and his band of plug-uglies do to gambling establishments. Mangano, No. 8 on the Chicago Crime Commission's list of 28 public enemies issued in May 1930, has had great success in this field.

Rocco Fischetti, alias John Senna, alias Charles Miller, has been reassigned to guard his cousin, John "Mimi" Capone, alias Arthur Colby, alias James Martin, brother of Al Capone.

Phil D'Andrea has been named chief "trouble shooter". He will make known to Skidmore names of policemen the gang want shifted in order to suit gang needs.

Ralph Pierce will continue to serve as body-guard for Humphries.

Ricca has an apartment in the 5300 block of West Jackson boulevard. He is known in the neighborhood as Paul De Lucia. A check-up revealed that Ricca has been a resident of Chicago for 14 years. Although a member of the Capone gang ever since his arrival, he has managed to get by without acquiring a criminal record. However, detectives have seized him on several occasions, only for him to regain his freedom promptly. His promotion to leadership created surprise in under-world circles.

Immigration records for this district reveal that Francesco Raffele Nitto, now Frank Nitti, was born at Augori, Italy, January 27, 1889, and entered the United States as an alien on or about July 1, 1891, arriving at New York City on the steamship *Guerra*. The records state:

He applied for declaration of intention, No. 129102 on March 9, 1921, and was naturalized as a citizen of

the United States on February 25, 1925, being issued
naturalization certificate No. 191944.

Nitti is a first cousin of Al Capone. He served
14 months of an 18-month sentence at the federal
penitentiary at Leavenworth, having pleaded guilty
to defrauding the government of income taxes
amounting to $158,828 plus interest. On
December 19, 1932, detectives Harry Lang and
Harry Miller, together with other officers, burst in
on Nitti and followers occupying room 554 in the
La Salle-Wacker Building, 221 North La Salle
Street. During the raid Nitti was shot three times.

Lang suffered a bullet wound into the arm.
Nitti charged Lang had wounded him, then
wounded himself in an effort to make it appear
Nitti had started to shoot it out with the officers.
Following his recovery he disappeared and
charges against Lang were dropped "for want of
prosecution".

Humphries, Jack Guzik, De Grazia and Ralph
Capone also have served sentences in federal pris-
ons for income-tax evasion.

On October 10, 1931, Phil D'Andrea was
seized in federal court during the trial of the "big
shot of big shots"—Al Capone. D'Andrea had a
loaded revolver in his belt. A bailiff's star and pen-
ciled letter requesting transfer of a patrolman to the
detective bureau were found in his possession.
Judge James H. Wilson thereupon found D'Andrea

guilty of contempt of court and consigned him to jail where he remained six months. The judge intimated that the next time he presided at the trial of a hoodlum he would ask that the United States army be called out.

Rocco De Grazia once operated 18 handbooks [used for recording offtrack racing bets] in Melrose Park.

"Dago Lawrence" Mangano has moved from 5929 Flourney Street to a Loop hotel. The police have nabbed him about 200 times. He has a summer cottage at Berrien Springs, Michigan.

[February 14, 1939]

CAPONE MOBSTERS ARE IN POWER ON TENTH ANNIVERSARY OF ST VALENTINE'S DAY MASSACRE OF THE MORAN GANG

Ten years after they had massacred seven Moran gangsters on Valentine's Day, Capone mobsters are still riding high, wide and handsome. Al Capone is in a federal hospital after serving a stretch at Alcatraz, but his lieutenants are in right with the Kelly-Nash machine. Working with William R. "Billy" Skidmore, the Capone mobsters have organized gambling to a degree of efficiency hitherto unknown in the city's history. Not satisfied with gambling, they dabble in organized vice, in carbonated beverages, in breweries, slot machines, and cut themselves into night clubs and any other form of enterprise where a show of muscle, smiled upon by the police, will count them in. A new figure of importance, one Paul Ricca, just a hanger-on in the mob 10 years ago, has risen to share front rank with Frank "The Enforcer" Nitti, "Little New York" Campagna, Jack Guzik and other leaders.

FBI Correspondence, February 1939– November 1956

To Director, FBI, Washington DC

February 21, 1939

Dear Sir,

In connection with the recent hold-up of a hotel in Miami, wherein a large sum of money, jewels, etc. was obtained, I am forwarding herewith a copy of a letter which was received by the City Editor of the *Chicago Daily News* and which copy was turned over to the writer by Francis Connor, a reporter for that paper.

The article that it refers to which Frank Nitti did not like was an article pertaining to the St Valentine's Day massacre which appeared in the

Chicago Daily News on February 14, 1939, and which article was written by Francis Connor.

D. M. LADD
Special Agent in Charge
FBI Chicago

To City Editor, Chicago Daily News

February 16, 1939

Nitti did not like that story you had in Tuesday's paper. He called a meeting last night at his home on the island. All the Capone boys that are here like Humphreys, Charlie Fischetti, by the way, they used his wife's car in the stickup here yesterday, they got $175,000. The coppers gave them a pass. Here they got the chief of police on the payroll here 'cause they operate here also. Nitti ordered all the boys back home to go for Kelly 100% to beat Courteney. They kicked in 50G [$50,000] already for Kelly.

Why don't you print that story you got, a copy was sent to *Look* magazine, it's the truth.

AN EX-WAITER FOR "CAPONE KILLERS"
[*Postmark Miami Beach, Florida*]

To J. Edgar Hoover, FBI, Washington DC

March 22, 1941

Dear Mr Hoover,

I received a letter a few days ago from Mrs Marion Stingley. She stated in her letter that Nelson Smith told her father that he was a witness to the St Valentine's massacre in Chicago, Illinois. Nelson Smith also told a woman, Mrs Bertha Raleigh, the same thing in the place Mrs Bertha Raleigh's husband was working for Nelson Smith there. Nelson Smith was painting cars there at that time that was in 1933. He told Will Sippel that they never caught the man who did the killing. I am sure he was the man that was the killer for that gang. Mr Smith has 12 bullet holes in his body. He has a silver plate the size of a 50-cent piece in the back of his head. He had the back of his head shot out with a 45-caliber revolver. He belonged to a gang in East St Louis and Detroit, Michigan and Chicago, Illinois. He puts Mexicans out to sell marijuana. He gets his marijuana in Denver, Colorado from a Mexican named Louie. Louie's woman's name is Paula.

Smith claims he has a son named Steve Smith and Steve's wife's name is Marie. Their names are in the board show magazine. Sometimes their names appear in the Chicago edition and New York. They are supposed to be stage dancers. Mr Nelson Smith can talk Spanish, Mexican and French. He is known as Two-gun Frenchie. His right name is Kenneth Nelson Smith. He is supposed to be married to Ruby Bridgeford at 231 Player Street, Marshalltown, Iowa. Nelson Smith is a spray painter. He paints cars and farm buildings.

F. L. Bridgeford is a building contractor at Marshalltown, Iowa. The chief of police Harold

Block is crooked. He protects Nelson in all his crooked ways because he pays his protection to keep from being arrested. There's another police officer, Glen Gooding, that is on the Marshalltown police force that tips Nelson Smith off on raids and told Smith he was run out of Kentucky so Nelson Smith told me. I was married to Nelson Smith until July 20, 1939.

Nelson Smith told me that Glen Gooding was running with a woman by the name of Helen Holman in Marshalltown, Iowa. Smith told me that Glen Gooding had paid for two illegal operations for Helen Holman in Des Moines, Iowa. I know Nelson Smith paid for an illegal operation for Ruby Clan on 2 July at the Deaconess Hospital at Marshalltown, Iowa in 1936. That's the woman that busted Nelson Smith up. He claims he isn't married to her, but I see by the Marshalltown paper that L. Dennis issued a building permit to Smith on 800 6th Street and F. L. Bridgeford is going to build the house for her.

Nelson Smith committed the act in Guyman, Oklahoma in the fall 1930. He bought an Oldsmobile 1926 two-door coach from the Guyman Motor Co and paid for it, and he traded it in Amarillo Texas December 28, 1930 for a model T coupe. He took the serial number off of the Oldsmobile and traded it off.

Nelson Smith, Roy Wilcox and Will Dee at Marshalltown, Iowa were mixed up in a land stealing deal in 1938. Will Dee went to the pen for two years, and Smith and Wilcox got out of the deal without taking a jail sentence.

MARGEURITE E. SMITH
Sterling
Colorado

Telegram to J. Edgar Hoover, FBI

August 5, 1948

Would greatly appreciate confirmation by you of names of men killed in Valentine Day massacre, Chicago: Adam Heyer, Peter Gusenberg, Frank Gusenberg, Frank Clark, John May, Albert Weinshank, Dr Reinhardt M. Schwimmer. Was Frank Foster an alias of Dr Schwimmer? Many thanks for your cooperation. Please wire reply collect.

TILLIE W. GREEN
Cosmopolitan *Magazine*
New York

To Miss Tillie W. Green, Cosmopolitan *Magazine,*
New York

Reference your telegram August 5. St Valentine's Day massacre involved no federal violation and was not investigated by FBI. Since information we have was not verified by FBI it is suggested you communicate directly with Chicago police authorities.

JOHN EDGAR HOOVER
Director FBI

*Memorandum of the US Government
to Mr Nichols*

November 28, 1956

From: M.A. Jones
Re: St Valentine's Day Massacre

There are attached excerpts concerning the above case taken from *The FBI Story, a Report to the People*, by Don Whitehead, published by Random House, 1956. These excerpts are from page 145 of the book. The full text of the book may be found in the FBI Library.

Interest in relating science to crime investigations picked up momentum in 1929. In that year the FBI began assembling a library of scientific books and papers dealing with subjects related to crime investigations, such as the testing of drugs, blood and hair. And, oddly enough, a gangland massacre spurred the development in Chicago. It was the so-called St Valentine's Day massacre.

This slaughter occurred on February 14, 1929. Members of the Al Capone gang, disguised as police, cornered seven persons, one of whom was believed to be "Bugs" Moran, in a garage. They stood their victims against a wall and mowed them down with machine-gun fire. During the coroner's jury investigation, some of the jurors asked what purpose was served in keeping the bullets found at the garage. Chicago police explained that ballistics experts could determine whether the bullets had been fired from certain guns—but that the Chicago Police Department had no laboratory in which to do such work.

POSTSCRIPT

[*Chicago Sunday Times*, February 14, 1937]

COINCIDENCE AND THE VALENTINE MASSACRE

The old adage that truth is stranger than fiction was never more grimly brought out than in the cold-blooded premeditated massacre of seven men eight years ago this St Valentine's Day and the coincidental fiction story that preceded it by only 12 days.

The story, *Hooch*, written by Charles Francis Coe, dealt with exactly the same situation that existed among the rival gangs at the time. The part referred to here appeared as the last instalment in the *Saturday Evening Post*, of February 2, 1929, a little more than a week before the fiction so coincidentally became fact.

The mind of the author conceived what he thought was sheer fiction but less than a week after his story was printed Gangland proved that they had minds with more imagination, capable of bigger and better things. Where Coe, in fiction, had dared to murder four men, Gangland, in reality, went three better, slicing down seven in their mad lust for power, two of whom were innocent.

The subject is that red stain on Chicago's map known to the world as St Valentine's Day massacre. The time was 10 o'clock on the cold morning of February 14, 1929, in a grease-grimed garage at 2122 North Clark Street. Seven men lounged about in the North Clark Street garage, headquarters of the "Bugs" Moran gang's illicit beer running activities. Five of them were hoodlums, yeomen of George "Bugs" Moran. They were Peter and Frank Gusenberg, Albert Weinshank, Adam Heyer and James Clark. The sixth was the garage mechanic, John May. The seventh was Dr Reinhardt H. Schwimmer, a dentist, who, for some strange reason, enjoyed the company of these rum runners.

Suddenly a long car drove up, stopped at the curb outside the garage. It looked like a detective bureau squad car. Five men got out—one in a policeman's uniform. Leisurely they lifted two wicked looking machine guns from the car, and leisurely they crossed the walk to the garage door.

Inside, the seven loungers jumped to their feet, tense, frightened. Then a smile crossed their faces as they glimpsed the man in the uniform of a "copper". Evidently, they thought, the boys from the Bureau were making another routine raid. The five men herded the seven toward the end of the room. They offered no resistance. "Line up against the wall!" they were ordered. They lined up. "Put your hands up!" came a second order. Fourteen hands reached for the ceiling. Probably a few of the hoodlums smiled. They apparently expected to be frisked for guns, as they had been so many times before. The third order came, "Turn around and face the wall!"

Those were the last words those seven men ever heard. A second later a stinging hail of machine gun slugs cut them down. Blood splashed on the wall, gathered in pools on the floor, flowed in long thin streams from seven corpses toward the drain. The executioners strolled out nonchalantly, hopped into their car and sped away.

Police and newspapermen were stunned at the sight that met their eyes in the dim light of the garage. The whole world was stunned later when news services flashed the story around the globe. Headlines screamed "Gangland Graduates from Murder to Massacre". The case climaxed Chicago's reputation as a hoodlum stamping ground.

Two blocks away "Bugs" Moran almost choked over his breakfast when he heard the news. "Only Capone would do a thing like that!" he muttered as he hastily packed his bag to blow town.

Capone was blamed. Capone was always blamed for everything. Many of his men were named, three, John Scalise, Albert Anselmi and "Machine Gun" Jack McGurn, were formally accused but were never brought to trial. The coroner's jury returned a verdict after long deliberations and investigation of "Murder by persons unknown".

Of all the strange angles and aspects of the Valentine massacre, perhaps the strangest is that the story called *Hooch* appeared only 12 days before and describes the massacre so accurately it might have been written after February 14.

Excerpt:

> Poppolipis stated, "We might as well look facts in the face. There is no room for Mitchell, Baer or Flenger." Zuroto laughed softly, "It is the truth. The funny thing about a murder charge is that it can't get any worse. You get just as much for bumping one man as you would an army."

> Slenk held the bottle before the headlight where all could see. "That's a good looking wrapper," he

admitted. He pulled the wrapper off the bottle and again held it up that the label might be inspected. "The labels ain't so good," he complained. "There's something about them that looks too new. I was telling Paddy the other day we ought to make up a Canadian Liquor Commission Stamp."

Marty spoke up: "It'd add about three bucks a bottle to the price we could get." Someone tried the side door. All three men whirled sharply.

"Who is it?" Mart asked throatily.

Slenk said "I'll find out."

"You better shut off them headlights," Baer suggested.

"Leave them on," Slenk said, "wait a minute. This ain't nothin."

He walked across the garage and opened the spring lock. Flenger stepped into the place. Slenk kicked the door shut.

"Where are they?" Flenger asked.

Before anyone could make answer the whole world seemed to explode about them. Dashes of flame cut through the gloom of the place. The terrific roar of shotguns and the mad scream of a machine gun ripped and shattered the silence.

Flenger fell in his tracks. Mitchell reeled back between the glowing headlights of the second truck, spread his arms over the radiator in an effort to keep himself on his feet, then groaned and sagged to the floor. Baer whirled uncertainly, sank to his knees with a curse and hurled the remnant of the whiskey bottle in the general direction of the last flash he had seen.

It was Slenk who stood longest against the barrage of the rum killers. A shadowy figure started around the end of the second truck. In his hands he carried a baby machine gun. A hoarse laugh crossed his lips. Calmly while Slenk watched him, terror in his eyes, the man lifted the gun, trained it upon him, and again the wild scream of 1,500 shots a minute tore at the walls of the garage.

It was over within a matter of seconds. After the deafening roar of the guns silence came suddenly. A whisper here, the scraping of a foot there, hoarse and labored breathing.

Then the side door of the building opened again. The calm night air swept in over four prone figures. Shadowy figures passed through the door, then along the alley beside the garage, finally to leap into a big motor car.

No one was ever convicted for the murders on St Valentine's Day, but the massacre did stop the growth of "Bugs" Moran's interests. He ultimately lived out the rest of his days in prison. Al Capone was released from Alcatraz in 1939 due to ill-health. From being the crime czar of Chicago—reputedly worth $100,000,000 at the height of his power—he died a powerless recluse in Florida in 1947.

New titles in the series

The Compendiums

Each book in this handsome series consists of three key historical accounts, and is illustrated with maps and contemporary photographs.

The World War I Collection

The official inquiry into the disastrous military campaign at Gallipoli, plus the despatches of British generals at the front during the first nine months of the war, are presented here.

The Dardanelles Commission, 1914–16

Examines why, when British troops were already heavily deployed in France, the leaders of the day saw fit to launch a major offensive in the eastern Mediterranean.

British Battles of World War I, 1914–15

A collection of despatches written by British commanders in the field, mainly in northern France.

ISBN 0 11 702466 X   418 pp plus 8 pp photographs
Price UK £14.99 US $19.95

The World War II Collection

Consists of three accounts of major milestones of World War II, written by the statesmen and military leaders of the day.

War 1939: Dealing with Adolf Hitler

Describes the policies of both Hitler and the British government in the months leading up to the outbreak of war.

D Day to VE Day: General Eisenhower's Report

General Eisenhower's personal account of the invasion of Europe, from June 1944 to May 1945.

The Judgment of Nuremberg, 1946

Focuses on the first trial of 21 major war criminals. The text describes the entire history, purpose and method of the Nazi party.

ISBN 0 11 702463 5   632 pp plus 8 pp photographs
Price UK £14.99 US $19.95

The Siege Collection

The stories of four sieges involving British troops in the days of British Empire are presented here.

The Siege of Kars, 1855

This little-known siege lasted five months and took place during the Crimean War, in the mountains of eastern Turkey.

The Boer War: Ladysmith and Mafeking, 1900

Contains despatches describing the siege and relief of both Ladysmith and Mafeking, as reported by the commanders in the field. The reverses suffered at Spion Kop are included.

The Siege of the Peking Embassy, 1900

Tells the story of how the diplomatic staff in Peking, China, were besieged by the Boxers in 1900. The despatches describe how the diplomats were rescued, while the personal diary of the British ambassador in Peking gives an extraordinary account of bravery in the face of extreme danger.

ISBN 0 11 702464 3   438 pp plus 8 pp photographs
                              Price UK £14.99 US $19.95

Tragic Journeys

Features three of the most tragic journeys the 20th century.

The Loss of the Titanic, 1912

The official inquiry presented here is the same report that was published in 1912. Also included is a reappraisal of the evidence relating to the SS *Californian*, the ship that failed to come to the rescue of the *Titanic*.

R.101: The Airship Disaster, 1930

In its heyday, the airship R.101 was considered as glamorous as the *Titanic*. Sadly, its fate was equally tragic, as she crashed on her maiden flight to India. The official inquiry investigates why it all went so disastrously wrong.

The Munich Air Crash, 1958

Eight key players from the Manchester United football team died in this tragic accident at Munich airport in 1958. Included here are the official inquiries into the causes.

ISBN 0 11 702465 1   350 pp plus 8 pp photographs
                              Price UK £14.99 US $19.95

The War Facsimiles

The War Facsimiles are exact reproductions of illustrated books that were published during the war years. They were produced by the British government to inform people about the progress of the war and the home-defence operations.

The Battle of Britain, August–October 1940

On 8 August 1940, the Germans launched the first of a series of mass air attacks on Britain in broad daylight. For almost three months, British and German aircraft were locked in fierce and prolonged combat in what has become known as the Battle of Britain. In 1941 the government published *The Battle of Britain* to explain the strategy and tactics behind the fighting that had taken place high in the sky over London and south-east England. Such was the public interest in this document, with its graphic maps and photographs, that sales had reached two million by the end of the war.

ISBN 0 11 702536 4   Price £4.99 US $8.95

The Battle of Egypt, 1942

Often referred to as the Battle of El Alamein, this battle was one of the major turning points for the Allies in World War II. The British, commanded by General Montgomery, were defending Egypt while the Germans under Rommel were attacking. This was a campaign the British could not afford to lose, because not only would it leave Egypt wide open for invasion, but it would also mean the loss of the Suez Canal and the oil fields. First published in 1943, *The Battle of Egypt* is an astonishing contemporary report of one of the most famous military victories in British history.

ISBN 0 11 702542 9   Price £5.99 US $10.95

Bomber Command: the Air Ministry account of Bomber Command's offensive against the Axis, September 1939–July 1941

Churchill declared on 22 June 1941: "We shall bomb Germany by day as well as by night in ever-increasing measure." Bomber Command of the RAF was to translate those words into action, beginning its attacks on Germany in May 1940, and steadily increasing its efforts as the war progressed. Published in 1941 at the height of World War II, *Bomber Command* tells the story of this fighting force during those early years.

ISBN 0 11 702540 2   Price £5.99 US $11.95

East of Malta, West of Suez: the Admiralty account of the naval war in the eastern Mediterranean, September 1939 to March 1941

This is the story of the British Navy in action in the eastern Mediterranean from September 1939 to March 1941 and their bid to seize control. During this time British supremacy was vigorously asserted at Taranto and Matapan. This facsimile edition contains contemporary maps, air reconnaissance photographs of the fleets and photographs of them in action.

ISBN 0 11 702538 0   Price £4.99 US $8.95

Fleet Air Arm: the Admiralty account of naval air operations, 1943

The Fleet Air Arm was established in 1939 as the Royal Navy's own flying branch. With its vast aircraft carriers bearing squadrons of fighter pilots, its main role was to protect a fleet or convoy from attack, or to escort an air striking force into battle. In *Fleet Air Arm*, published in 1943, the public could read for the first time of the expeditions of these great ships as they pursued and sank enemy warships such as the *Bismarck*.

ISBN 0 11 702539 9   Price £5.99 US $11.95

Land at War: the official story of British farming 1939–1944

Land at War was published by the Ministry of Information in 1945 as a tribute to those who had contributed to the war effort at home. It explains how 300,000 farms, pinpointed by an extensive farm survey, had been expected to increase their production dramatically, putting an extra 6.5 million acres of grassland under the plough. This is a book not just about rural life, but of the determination of a people to survive the rigours of war.

ISBN 0 11 702 537 2   Price £5.99 US $11.95

Ocean Front: the story of the war in the Pacific, 1941–44

Ocean Front tells the story of the Allies' war against Japan in the central and western Pacific. Starting with Pearl Harbor in December 1941, this fascinating book recounts the Allies' counter-offensive, from the battles of the Coral Sea and Midway, to the recapture of the Aleutian Islands and the final invasion of the Philippines. Illustrated throughout with amazing photographs of land and sea warfare, *Ocean Front* provides a unique record of the American, Australian and New Zealand fighting forces in action.

ISBN 0 11 702543 7   Price £5.99 US $11.95

Roof over Britain: the official story of Britain's anti-aircraft defences, 1939–1942

Largely untold, *Roof over Britain* is the story of Britain's ground defences against the attacks of the German air force during the Battle of Britain in the autumn of 1940. First published in 1943, it describes how the static defences – the AA guns, searchlights and balloons – were organised, manned and supplied in order to support the work of the RAF.

ISBN 0 11 702541 0   Price £5.99 US $11.95

Uncovered editions: how to order

FOR CUSTOMERS IN THE UK
Ordering is easy. Simply follow one of these five ways:

Online
Visit www.clicktso.com

By telephone
Please call 0870 600 5522, with book details to hand.

By fax
Fax details of the books you wish to order (title, ISBN,
quantity and price) to: 0870 600 5533.
Please include details of your credit/debit card plus
expiry date, your name and address and telephone
number, and expect a handling charge of £3.00.

By post
Post the details listed above (under 'By fax') to:
The Stationery Office
PO Box 29
Norwich NR3 1GN
You can send a cheque if you prefer by this method
(made payable to The Stationery Office). Please include
a handling charge of £3 on the final amount.

TSO bookshops
Visit your local TSO bookshop (or any good bookshop).

FOR CUSTOMERS IN THE UNITED STATES
Uncovered editions are available through all major
wholesalers and bookstores, and are distributed to the
trade by Midpoint Trade Books.
Phone 913 831 2233 for single copy prepaid orders
which can be fulfilled on the spot, or simply for more
information.
Fax 913 362 7401